ORTHODOX SPIRITUALITY

ORTHODOX SPIRITUALITY

*An Outline of the Orthodox
Ascetical and Mystical
Tradition*

By
A MONK OF THE
EASTERN CHURCH

Second Edition

Published for
THE FELLOWSHIP OF SS. ALBAN AND SERGIUS

LONDON
SPCK

First published 1945
Second edition 1978

SPCK
Holy Trinity Church
Marylebone Road
London NW1 4DU

PRINTED IN GREAT BRITAIN BY
WILLIAM CLOWES & SONS LIMITED, LONDON, BECCLES AND COLCHESTER

ISBN 0 281 03589 X

CONTENTS

PREFACE TO THE SECOND EDITION

THIS BOOK is in two parts : the first is a faithful reproduction of an edition published in 1945. The second is an appendix, bringing up to date (to 1977) the earlier work.

That first edition included a bibliography which was adequate at the time. Since it is now out of date, it is not reproduced here. An up-to-date bibliography would unduly lengthen a short book, which should remain such. Readers who would like more detailed information are advised to consult the excellent though elementary bibliography to be found in the book *The Orthodox Church* by Timothy Ware (Penguin 1969). They might also get in touch with the Fellowship of St. Alban and St. Sergius, whose secretariat publishes book lists and is ready to give up-to-date information about books and periodicals concerning Orthodox spirituality (St. Basil's House, 52 Ladbroke Grove, London WII 2PB).

INTRODUCTION

THIS BOOK IS neither a scholarly history of Orthodox spirituality, nor a far-searching theological treatise on ascetical and
mystical graces, nor a description of the psychology of
Orthodox mystics, but a short and very simple introduction
to the *first principles* of the spirituality of the Eastern
Orthodox Church.

The spiritual life is here considered in the light of the
doctrine of the Eastern Orthodox Church. This name
applies to the "sister-Churches" whose faith is expressed by
the decisions of the seven Œcumenical Councils, and who
maintain communion with the Patriarchate of Constantinople
and the Apostolic Sees of Antioch, Alexandria and Jerusalem.
The Orthodox Church, as a Church, has a definite teaching
on ascetical and mystical questions, and this teaching is a
tradition (*paradosis*), handed down from the birth of
Christianity to our own days. It is this tradition, and not
the personal theories, either of himself or of any arbitrarily
chosen spiritual writer, however great, that the author has
here tried to set forth.

Where is it possible to find the genuine and, if one may use
the word, official expression of this tradition ? There are
four main sources: first, the Word of God laid down in the
Holy Scripture ; secondly, the definitions of the Councils,
which, because of their dogmatic importance, are sign-posts
along the paths of spiritual life ; thirdly, the liturgical
texts ; and, lastly, the writings of the Fathers.

If the authority of certain Fathers were to be placed
in the foreground (just as Dom C. Butler, in his
Western Mysticism, singled out St. Augustine, St. Gregory
the Great and St. Bernard), it would be in accordance
with the tradition of the Eastern Church to prefer the
three Bishops whom our liturgical texts call "the holy

pontiffs and œcumenical doctors" : St. John Chrysostom, who had no theology of his own, but simply the theology of everybody in the Church, or, in other words, the theology of the Church itself ; St. Basil the Great, whose monastic rules safely guided the spiritual life of millions of men ; and St. Gregory Nazianzen, rightly named "the Theologian", of whom Rufinus of Aquileia wrote : "Not to agree with Gregory's faith is a manifest proof of error in the faith." [1] From such Masters and Fathers in Christ, not from modern philosophers or novelists, even though they had the religious genius of Khomiakov, Dostoievsky and Berdyaev, and not even from the spiritual "elders" of Athos or Optina, whose views remain private opinions, we shall *authoritatively* learn the Orthodox way to holiness.

These Masters are common to East and West, although they had greater influence upon the East. It cannot be too often repeated : there is no chasm between Eastern and Western Christianity. The fundamental principles of Christian spirituality are the same in the East and in the West ; the methods are very often alike ; the differences do not bear on the chief points. On the whole, there is *one* Christian spirituality with, here and there, some variations of stress and emphasis.

The whole teaching of the Latin Fathers may be found in the East, just as the whole teaching of the Greek Fathers may be found in the West. Rome has given St. Jerome to Palestine. The East has given Cassian to the West and holds in special veneration that Roman of the Romans, Pope St. Gregory the Great (our Gregory Dialogos). St. Basil would have acknowledged St. Benedict of Nursia as his brother and heir. St. Macrina would have found her sister in St. Scholastica. St. Alexis "the man of God," the "poor man under the stairs," has been succeeded by the wandering beggar St. Benedict Labre. St. Nicholas would

[1] *P.G.* xxxvi, 736.

have felt as very near to him the burning charity of St. Francis of Assisi and St. Vincent de Paul. St. Seraphim of Sarov would have seen the desert blossoming under Father Charles de Foucauld's feet, and would have called St. Thérèse of Lisieux "my joy".

In the same way the Eastern Church can value the achievements of "evangelical" Christians. She can acknowledge and honour all that is so deeply Christian—and therefore "Orthodox"—in such men as (to name only a few) George Fox, Nicholas Zinzendorf, John Wesley, William Booth, the Sadhu Sundar Singh.

In the Church of England, John Mason Neale was deeply sensitive to the innermost Greek piety, and interpreted it beautifully in his hymnodic translations. He seems to have been, to a large extent, a Greek soul. Two Anglican priests who have died recently, though they differed greatly from each other, were both of them Eastern spiritual types: Father William, the saintly hermit of Glasshampton, and C. F. Andrews, the servant of India, who shone with the steady light of Christ. On the other hand, one of the greatest ascetics and mystics of the Orthodox Church, St. Tikhon Zadonsky, who was conversant with Latin scholasticism and quoted St. Augustine, seems to have read the Anglican Joseph Hall (Bishop of Norwich) and the German pietist Johann Arndt. A genuine and intense spiritual life is the shortest and safest way to re-union. The author hopes that this little book—which was written partly in the house of the Community of St. John the Evangelist at Cowley, partly in that of the Community of the Resurrection at Mirfield, partly in a Settlement of the Society of Friends at Woodbrooke (Selly Oak), and which is indebted to Dom Gregory Dix for many useful suggestions—may bear witness to the treasures held in common by Churches whose ways have parted. It is offered to the Fellowship of SS. Sergius and Alban. The Fellowship has known Orthodox spirituality mainly through Russian channels. Its members will find here some perspectives to which they are less accustomed. Orthodox tradition is wider than any particular country and culture. It is to the Greek and near-Eastern (Palestinian, Syrian, Egyptian) tradition, which is more ancient than the Russian, that reference will chiefly be made. But the debt of Orthodoxy, and indeed of the whole Christian world, to Russian holiness and love, and to the Church of the Russian martyrs and confessors must also be emphasized.

The author desires to record his gratitude to Archbishop Germanos of Thyateira, who has most kindly read this book in manuscript and suggested certain improvements.

This work is humbly submitted to the judgment of the praying Church of Christ. *Si quid male dixi, totum relinquo correctioni Ecclesiae.*

CHAPTER I

THE HISTORICAL DEVELOPMENT OF ORTHODOX SPIRITUALITY

IN ITS PRESENT STATE, orthodox spirituality is the result of nineteen centuries of evolution: an evolution to which various ethnic and cultural factors have contributed (Palestine, Syrian, Hellenism, Slavism, etc.) but whose homogeneity has been secured by a common Christian faith. The elements that has been revealed successively in the course of this evolution must not be conceived as superimposed layers, each of which finishes where another begins. They are, rather, dynamic streams, rising one after another ; they diverge, cross one another, meet, and continue down to the present time.

We may distinguish, in the development of Orthodox spirituality, six main elements : the Scriptural element ; the primitive Christian element ; the intellectual element ; the early monastic element ; the liturgical element ; and the "technical-contemplative" element.

(1) *The Scriptural element*

The Word of God present in the holy and divinely inspired Scriptures remains the foundation of the whole of Orthodox spirituality. "Sanctify them through Thy truth : Thy Word is truth" (John 17. 17). In Orthodox churches the Book of the Gospels always lies on the middle of the altar, and, while no mark of worship is paid to the reserved Eucharistic elements (when, as is not necessarily the case, they are reserved), each priest approaching the holy Table kisses the Gospel first. The Holy Scripture is the very substance of the dogmas and liturgies of the Orthodox Church and, through them, impregnates the piety of Ortho-dox souls. This is so obvious that one need not insist upon it.

But, besides this central point, some secondary points deserve to be raised.

The Orthodox Church can be called a "Biblicist" Church. She has always recommended and encouraged the reading of the Holy Book. In the fourth century, St. John Chrysostom was the stubborn champion of assiduous Bible reading, even among the laity. There is found among the simplest Orthodox folk a personal and intimate intercourse with the Gospel. Harnack, who saw in Orthodoxy a mixture of Greek metaphysics and ritualism, nevertheless emphasized this fact : "Jesus' words . . . take the first place in this Church too, and the quiet mission which they pursue is not suppressed. : . . They are read in private and in public, and no superstition avails to destroy their power. Nor can its fruits be mistaken by anyone who will look below the surface. Among these Christians, too, priests and laity, there are men who have come to know God as the Father of mercy and the leader of their lives, and who love Jesus Christ, not because they know Him as the person with two natures, but because a ray of His Being has shone from the Gospel into their hearts, and this ray has become light and warmth to their own lives. . . . I need only refer again to Tolstoi's *Village Tales*."[1]

Certain books of the Bible have had a particular influence on Orthodox spirituality.

Psalms hold a great place in public worship, and, since the time of the Desert Fathers, have fed individual monastic piety. Certain psalms in their entirety, or at least fragments of them, haunt Orthodox memories (e.g. the six introductory psalms of the evening service, or Psalm 51). Even among people who are practically detached from the Church some words of the psalms, learnt during their childhood, often give a concrete shape to a longing for God.

[1] A. Harnack, *What is Christianity?* transl. by T. Bailey Saunders (London, 1901), pp. 242–243.

The synoptic Gospels have deeply entered the Orthodox popular conscience. The simple and unconditional precepts of the Sermon on the Mount, and the call of Christ to all them that suffer and are heavy laden, have found a special echo there. These Gospel passages lie at the base of what has been called "the Russian Kenoticism." One should understand under that name not a particular theology of the *kenosis* (in the technical meaning of the word), but a singularly vivid awareness of all that the "humiliation of Christ" and His "taking the form of a servant" (Phil. 2. 7) imply. The self-lowering of our Lord, meditated upon by simple and ardent souls, gave birth to a special kind of asceticism, not unknown in the West but more proper to the East : the ascetic way of the "fool for Christ's sake" (the Greek *salos*, the Slavonic *yurodiv*). Non-resistance to violence, exemplified in ancient Russian history by the Holy Princes Boris and Gleb before being systematized by Tolstoi, belongs to the same trend. A kind of connaturality between the Russian soul and suffering has produced, in the name of Christ, a passionate pity and generosity towards all the "humiliated and offended." This breaking of a compassionate heart comes over and over again in almost all Russian literature, chiefly in Dostoievsky's novels.

St. John Chrysostom has been the special interpreter of the Apostle Paul to the Greek-speaking East as was St. Augustine to the Latin West. Both of them deeply entered into St. Paul's thought concerning Christ's Mystical Body, but while Augustine mainly deduced from Paul a theology of grace, Chrysostom rather drew from him practical ways of life.

Has the fourth Gospel been the prevailing Scriptural influence on the Orthodox Church ? This has often been said. The "Johannine" character of Orthodoxy is supposed to contrast with the "Petrinism" and "Paulinism" of other Christain confessions. Such an idea seems to have origi-

nated in the romantic, religious atmosphere which surrounded both the Russian Slavophils and German exegesis
and philosophy round about the 'forties of the last century.
It has left lasting traces, recognizable, for instance, in
the *Peter and John* of Father Sergius Bulgakov and in the
Three Dialogues of Vladimir Soloviev (where Pope Peter II
represents the Roman Church, Professor Pauli, Protestantism, and the saintly elder John, Orthodoxy). It is true
that the Gospel according to St. John is held in great
veneration within the Orthodox Church. Thus its prologue
constitutes the Gospel lesson for the Easter night service.
The fourth Gospel has at the same time attracted simple,
pious souls by the sweetness of its radiance, and captivated
speculative intellects by the depth of its thought, and
by its Logos- and Light-metaphysics. It is well known
with what affection Origen pored over it. But the same
thing could be said of St. Augustine. On the one hand the
fourth Gospel has exercised on many of the Latin Fathers
and faithful exactly the same attraction which it did on
Greek Fathers and faithful of a kindred spiritual type. On
the other hand, if one considers the Greek Fathers as a whole,
it does not appear that the fourth Gospel has moulded their
thoughts more than have the other writings of the New
Testament.

Through the whole evolution of Orthodox thought, the
two attitudes towards Scripture which already existed in the
third century can be traced : the literalist and historicist
attitude of the School of Antioch, and the allegorist and
speculative attitude of the School of Alexandria. Besides these
two attitudes, which are the attitudes of theologians, there
can be noticed all through Orthodox history the existence
of a spirituality which we might call "evangelical". This
spirituality takes care to identify Christian life neither with the
rigorous asceticism of the Desert, nor with ritual worship ;
it lays stress on the spirit and virtues of the Gospel, on the

necessity of following Christ, on charity towards the poor and afflicted. St. John Chrysostom is the most eminent representative of this trend. It prevailed in ancient Constantinopolitan monasticism, owing to the rules of St. Basil, who was both evangelically and humanistically minded, and of St. Theodore the Studite. The monks of Constantinople extended their "philanthropic" activities very far. This evangelical attitude found its most popular expression in the legend of St. Nicholas. It has assumed more precise historical features in the life of St. John the Almsgiver, Patriarch of Alexandria in the seventh century—the Orthodox St. Vincent de Paul—who had perpetually upon his lips the beautiful word *philochristos* and whose motto was "to be compassionate and to give alms."

In Russia itself, which has been too frequently called the land of all religious extremisms, this evangelical piety, consisting in simplicity, kindness, practical sense, trusting prayer, soberness and discretion, was represented by a long tradition of men venerated as saints : among them St. Sergius of Radonezh, the father of Moscovite monasticism in the fourteenth century ; St. Nil of Sorsk, the monastic reformer of the sixteenth century ; St. Tikhon of Zadonsk (1724–1783), the original of the holy monk Zosima in Dostoievsky's *The Brothers Karamazov* ; Bishop Theophan the Recluse (1815–1894), who constantly refers to St. John Chrysostom ; and, at the dawn of this century, Father John of Kronstadt. The Russian theologian M. Tareev (1866–1934) endeavoured, not without some impatience and lack of comprehension in regard to dogmas and rites, but in a sincere and stirring way, to work out a purely "evangelical" Orthodox theology and spirituality.

Such modern Church movements as *Zoe* in Greece, "the *Lord's Army* in Rumania, and the new "bogomils" in Bulgaria are, in the core, Evangelical Orthodox movements.

(2) *The "Primitive Christian" element*

By "primitive Christian" element we understand the
Christian atmosphere of the three first centuries, the complex of ideas and feelings proper to the Apostolic Fathers
and the Apologists before the great conciliar and dogmatic
period of the fourth century.   Such writings as the *Didache*,
the letters of St. Ignatius of Antioch, the Shepherd of
Hermas, the early Passions of the Martyrs and—not least—
the inscriptions and symbolic frescoes of the Catacombs,
help us to step into this atmosphere.

Martyrdom occupies the central place in Christian conceptions of this period.   The shedding of blood for the
Lord Jesus' sake is considered to be the normal and
desirable completion of every Christian life.   According to
Origen and Tertullian, the life of the Christian ought to be
a preparation for martyrdom.   Everybody is called to be an
"athlete" of the Lord.   If one has not the blessed happiness
to die for His Name, one may at least, suffer, be persecuted,
and perhaps tortured for His sake.   One is, in such case, a
"confessor".

The theme of martyrdom has never been absent from the
Orthodox Church.   During the centuries of oppression of
Orthodoxy by Islam, martyrs and confessors were numerous.
After the Russian Revolution, the Russian Church, red with
the blood of her martyrs, found herself back in the conditions
of the primitive Church.

When maryrdom or "confession" was wanting, one could
nevertheless be an "athlete" by heroically fighting against
human passions.   In this manner the "ascetics" obtained a
special place within the ancient Church before monasticism
was born.   "Ascetics" were characterized by poverty,
fasting and, above all, continence (*enkrateia*).   As early as
A.D. 110, virgins and widows are mentioned as a privileged
class in the Church of Smyrna.   Hermas and Justin speak of

them. The *Banquet of the Ten Virgins* by St. Methodius of Olympus (311) is an exaltation of virginity.[1] The Orthodox Church has followed this tradition.

A ferment of enthusiasm penetrates the whole Christian life during the era of persecutions. Martyrs and confessors were upheld by the joy of Christ's presence. "The Lord was standing near them (the martyrs) and conversing with them" as we read in the *Martyrdom of Polycarp*.[2] "Another will be in me who will suffer for me," said St. Felicitas.[3] They moved in an atmosphere of prophetic visions and revelations. Montanism was a deformation of this enthusiasm, just as Encratism was a deformation of the ideal of continence. The Orthodox Church fought against these excesses (revived later by the Paulicians and medieval Bogomils), but she keeps as her authentic and most precious treasure the radiance of joy in the Lord Jesus. St. Seraphim of Sarov, a century ago, used to call every one of his interlocutors "my joy"; one feels in this expression a wind from the spring times of Christianity.

The first Christians lived in the eschatological hope, in the fervent expectation of the Parousia. Orthodoxy maintains this attitude. To her, the life to come is not an appendix to the earthly life ; our earthly life is but an introduction to the eternal Kingdom. Orthodoxy is often charged with "other-worldliness". If this charge is justified, it is just such an other-worldliness as that which the first Christian generation expressed by the prayer : "Amen. Even so, come, Lord Jesus" (Rev. 22. 20).

(3) *The Intellectual Element*

The establishment of the *Didaskaleion* (school for catechumens) of Alexandria, in the third century, marks the beginnings not only of doctrinal elaboration, but of a speculative spirituality, which left a deep stamp on the Orthodox

---

[1] *P.G.* XVIII, 9–408.　　　　[2] *Martyr. Polycarp*, I, 19.
[3] Ruinart, *Acta primorum martyrum sincera et selecta*, p. 53.

Church. This spirituality owed much to another Alexandrian, Philo, who sought to combine Judaism and Platonism. He was the theoretician of contemplative life and of the Logos, and a master of allegorical exegesis.

The main features of Christian Alexandrianism are : a certain dualistic view of matter and spirit ; a leaning towards dialectic ; scriptural allegorism ; a method of abstraction which, being "apophatic" (negative) theology, sees in God the supremely Undeterminate, i.e. a theologizing by the way of negation or removal of human attributes ; finally a quest for salvation through the knowledge which the Logos imparts. In it we find all the materials of a philosophy and a theology, and of a spiritual life as well.

Clement and Origen wanted to oppose to heretical gnosticism a Christian gnosis. The "true gnosis" described by Clement is very near the idea of the Gospel. Clement writes :[1] "Our own gnosis . . . is our Saviour Himself." There is however in this conception of a twofold Christianity something which is alien to the Gospel, and Orthodoxy finally did not admit it.

The great Alexandrines were not merely intellectualists. They were also heroic ascetics. Origen wrote an *Exhortation to Martyrdom* and passionately longed for such an end. This allegorist could be quite a literalist when practice was concerned. Thus, having read the words "cut them off . . ." said of the members which offend (Matt. 18. 8), and the other words spoken of the men who "have made themselves eunuchs for the Kingdom of Heaven's sake (Matt. 19. 12), he deliberately mutilated himself. The loftiest Alexandrian speculations could make contact with popular piety. J. Quasten has recently shown the close links which Christian Hellenism established between the Logos theology and the symbol of the Good Shepherd.[2]

[1] *Stromateis* VI, 1.
[2] *Der Gute Hirte in hellenisticher und frühchristlicher Logostheologie* in *Heilige Ueberlieferung*, Maria Laach (Münster, 1938).

Clement, in the hymn which closes the *Pedagogue*, prays thus : "Be the guide, and Shepherd, of the *logical* sheep." The Logical sheep—the reasonable sheep—the sheep of the Logos. We have mentioned the Logos several times. It is difficult to realize the central place occupied by the Logos in Christian Greek thought and piety. As has been rightly said, what "reason" was for the eighteenth century, "science" for the nineteenth, and "life" for the beginning of the twentieth century, the *Logos*—at the same time intellect, divine word and first cosmic principle—was for the Hellenistic world, both heathen and Christian. Identified with Christ, the Logos is the medium between the Father and man, the light of the soul, the master of the inner life. Christian life consists in the perfect subjection to the Logos, a subjection not only of the mind but of the flesh as well. For, through the Incarnation "the flesh has become logified" (*sarkos logotheisēs*).[1]

It is St. Athanasius who speaks thus, of whom Heiler said : "The christological mysticism of Athanasius is the heart of the Eastern Church." [2] The dogmatic Fathers of the fourth century have been, indeed, precise and safe guides for Orthodox thought and piety. The Christological definitions of the Œcumenical Councils, completing what St. Irenaeus had written long before on the "recapitulation" of all men in Christ, have illuminated not only the beliefs but also the inner life of Christians. These conciliar formulæ may seem dry and remote from personal experience ; in reality the Chalcedonian Christology, in defining the relation between the divine and human natures in the Person of Christ, draws the main lines of the spiritual life of the man in whom Christ operates and who takes Christ as a pattern. Conciliar discussions about the words *homoousios* and *homoiousios*, and even the violences of

[1] Athanasius, *Orat. contra Arianos*, III, 33.
[2] F. Heiler, *Im Ringe um der Kirche*, 2nd ed. (Munich, 1931), p. 65.

Cyril of Alexandria, are to be explained by the fear of jeopardizing not only the objective truth, but also the subjective experience of that truth, and so the reproduction of the Incarnation in the humblest Christian. The writings of the pseudo-Areopagite (the *corpus dionyisiacum* saw the light in the fifth or sixth century) have influenced East and West equally. The non-authenticity of these writings and their close dependence on the writings of the heathen Proclus matter little. What does matter is the fact that the Christian Church acknowledged the orthodoxy and excellence of their doctrine. The pseudo-Dionysius introduced in the Church the notion of "mystical theology"; he understands by that name a supernatural and unspeakable intuition, as distinct from "apodeictic" or demonstrative theology. He develops a complete theory of the union with God (*theiahenosis*). It will suffice, for the time being, to keep in mind these two general ideas.

St. Maximus the Confessor (662) has been, in the Greek Church, the most authoritative commentator upon the pseudo-areopagitic teachings and a conspicuous representative of speculative spirituality. The interpenetration of his doctrine and his life is admirable. His glosses on Dionysius, his *Mystagogy*, his *Chapters on Charity* express the highest mysticism; but the same man who preaches our deification and the knowledge of the Trinity through contemplative prayer has also, in his *Ascetical Book*, set forth the simplest and most practical spiritual methods. He does not separate deification from ethics and asceticism. According to Maximus our deification is worked out by the identification of our human will with the divine will. Here we have a striking instance of the application of Christological dogma to the inner life: our Saviour, within Himself, constantly brought His human will under the subjection of His divine will; we ought, *mutatis mutandis*, to do the same. Maximus, who, in his fight against monothelitism, had much to suffer for the sake of the dogma of the two wills of Christ, took his Christology over into concrete life.

The Orthodox Church has often been called a Platonist Church. But as a Church, i.e. as the dispenser of divine revelation, she is not bound to any human philosophy. It is true that many Greek Fathers made use of a Platonic or neo-Platonic terminology, and manifested a warm sympathy towards the leading ideas of Platonism. But these Fathers themselves were Platonizers rather than Platonists. Moreover, we must not overlook or underrate an Aristotelian Orthodox tradition, which goes from St. John Damascene (eighth century) to Gennadios Scholarios (fifteenth century). Finally, as regards spirituality (and this is our present subject), we must notice that, if most of the Orthodox conceptions and terms relating to contemplation are inspired by Platonism, Orthodox ethics and asceticism have been for their part inspired by Aristotelianism and Stoicism.

The speculative and intellectualist stream has penetrated modern Orthodoxy. Greek theologians are on the whole traditionalist, strictly patristic, and even to a certain extent scholastic. But, from the time of Skovoroda (eighteenth century) Russian theologians such as Soloviev, Frank and Lossky have returned to the Alexandrian tradition and, not without contact and sometimes collusion with German idealism, have carried on what V. Ern called the "fight for the Logos" : Berdyaev occupies a special place, as he has been deeply influenced by Eckhart and the gnosis of Boehme. Paul Florensky and Bulgakov, who have developed into a systematic "sophiology" certain elements present in Soloviev's books, must also be set apart. We shall not insist on their doctrines concerning Holy Wisdom, first because they constitute much controverted *theologumena* (i.e. theological opinions only) and do not belong to the common teaching of the Church, with which we are concerned ; and secondly because they are more nearly related to dogmatics and philosophy than to spirituality. However, if theoretical sophiology goes beyond our field, it interests us in so far as it defines a certain spiritual attitude. The fact is that, in Florensky, Bulgakov, Ilyn, Zander, or the Rumanian Lucian Blaga, we can discern a "sophianic" attitude which might be defined as an acute perception of, and a communion with, the spiritual beauty of the world. It is the same feeling that led the Greeks to identify, in the word *kalokagathia*, the beautiful and the good. We find some reflection of it in the Greek term which describes the Good Shepherd: *ho poimēn ho kalos* "the Shepherd beautiful". This spiritual-æsthetical element is very strong in Orthodoxy.

On the whole, the intellectualism of the Greek Fathers and of Orthodoxy constitutes a climate of thought in which nobleness and harmony flourish. To the fine word of St. Augustine: *Ama valde intellectum*, the Greek world could reply with this saying of a fourth-century bishop, Synesius: "To be a Greek is to know how to commune with men," or the utterance of a twentieth-century Patriarch, the late Meletius, about "the hellenism of Golgotha crowning the hellenism of the Acropolis." In place of the clear-obscure of the philosophies or theologies of feeling, of the dark night with its flashes of lightning and peals of thunder, of Kierkegaard and Barth, Orthodoxy presents a classical landscape, bathed in the light of the Logos.

(4) *The Early Monastic Element*

We have already mentioned Constantinopolitan monasticism and associated with the "scriptural" element of Orthodoxy the discreet, charitable, purely evangelical tradition of St. Basil and St. Theodore the Studite. But we must take into account the influence brought to bear on Orthodoxy by another type of monasticism, i.e. the primeval monasticism of Egypt, Syria, and Palestine. The expression "Fathers of the Desert" sums up this aspect of monasticism. The Desert has spoken to the world through a series of writings of the fourth and following centuries : the *Vita Antonii*, the *Lausiac History* by Palladius, the *Apophthegms of the Fathers*, the *Spiritual Meadow* by John Moschus, the *Scale of Paradise* by St. John Climacus, the treatises of St. Nilus (or of the pseudo-Nilus), Isaac of Nineveh, Evagrius of the Pontus, Diadochus of Photike, the fifty homilies attributed to Macarius (the origin of these remarkable homilies is perhaps not Orthodox, but sectarian, either Messalian or Euchite ; they nevertheless comprise, in their essentials, a classic expression of Orthodox spirituality.) The *Collationes* of John Cassian form a link between the Eastern Desert and Western monasticism, the author having received in the East the traditions of the monastic Fathers and brought them to Southern Gaul.

When we make a distinction between the spirituality of the Desert and the "evangelical" monastic tradition of St. Basil, we certainly do not mean that the high holiness of the Desert has no roots in the Gospel. As a matter of fact we find, at the start of the "Desert movement", the same evangelical text and the same literal interpretation of it which moved St. Francis of Assisi to a total renunciation. According to the *Vita Antonii*, the young Antony, being in his twentieth year, once listened to the reading of the words : " If thou wilt be perfect, go and sell that thou hast, and give to the poor . . . and come and follow me" (Matt. 19. 21) ; and, leaving the world, he gave an example which many followed. But our Lord did not call the early monastic Fathers in order that they should follow Him in His missionary travels. He called them in order that they should follow Him as "led up of the Spirit into the wilderness" (Matt. 4. 1). He spoke to their ears and hearts the same words which God had spoken to Hosea about his erring wife : "I will bring her into the wilderness, and speak comfortably unto her" (Hos. 2. 14). Like Anna the prophetess, they "served God with fastings and prayers night and day" (Luke 2. 37), and they received the reward described in Isaiah (35. 1), "The wilderness and the solitary place shall be glad for them ; and the desert shall rejoice, and blossom as the rose."

The monasticism of the desert differs from Basilian or Benedictine monachism in obvious and somewhat marked ways. Separation from the world is rigorous. There is no "work for the world" such as land-clearing, education or social work ; or, more truly, the only work for the world is prayer. Monastic life is directed exclusively towards contemplation. Although St. Antony and St. Pachomius insist on discretion and measure, external austerities come into the foreground. Shenoute, for instance, is literally seeking to beat ascetical records. Fortitude, daring, generosity—the *prothumia* of which Antony spoke—become, if not the most important, at least the most apparent virtues. Notwithstanding the cenobitic (common life) organization of St. Pachomius, individual forms of monastic life (anchorites, stylites, dendrites or forest monks, etc.) prevail.

The Desert Fathers waged heroic fights against the powers of evil and darkness. The development of demonology in Christian spirituality is to a great extent due to their influence.

The type of prayer called *monologistos*, i.e. prayer consisting of one or a few words (the *oratio jaculatoria* of Western spirituality), was one of their favourite methods. The repetition of the psalm-verse *Deus, in adjutorium meum intende* in the West and the Jesus-prayer ("Lord Jesus Christ, Son of God, have mercy upon me a sinner") in the East both come from the Desert.

It is also in the Desert that the doctrine of contemplative life was evolved. We should observe that the Desert Fathers identify contemplative life, *bios theorētikos*, with apostolic life, *bios apostolikos*. By "apostolic life" they do not mean a life dedicated to the preaching of the Gospel, but monastic life itself, for there only was the ideal of fervent and communal life held by the primitive Church of Jerusalem kept up.

The Fathers of the Desert considered *apatheia* the supreme ideal. This word has been the cause of serious misunderstanding. It has often been translated by "apathy", "impassibility", "absence of passion" with the Stoic meaning of "insensibility". But the *apatheia* of the Fathers means something quite different from a kind of anæsthesia of the feelings. Their *apatheia* is the fruit of love or charity. It is, in reality, the state of a soul in which love towards God and men is so ruling and burning as to leave no room for human (self-centred) passions. Thus Diodorus of Photike was able to speak—at first sight paradoxically—of "the fire of *apatheia*".

Another mistake is to look upon the Desert Fathers as mere ascetics or penitents, closed to the intimate joys of mystical life. To say that they were not unacquainted with mystical experiences would be too little. Their daily life was accompanied by visions and contacts with the heavenly world. The secrets of the Desert were a foretaste of angelic beatitude. St. John Climacus speaks of the flames of love in terms which recall to mind the poems of St. John of the Cross. Cassian describes the "fiery prayer" (*ignita oratio*)

Yet another mistake is to think that the solitaries were uninterested in other men. Evagrius of Pontus says: "Better is a layman who serves his neighbour than an anchorite who has no compassion for his brother."[1]

Finally it was in the Desert that the idea of the director of conscience—the father or spiritual elder (*pater pneumatikos* of the Greeks, *starets* of the Slavs)—took shape.

[1] *Sentences, P.G.* XL, 1280.

The ideal of this primitive monasticism has remained in force within the Orthodox Church to this day. An Orthodox can hardly conceive of salvation without a certain severance from the world, without a complete self-denial. He hardly conceives of the religious life under other forms than the life of Mary who chose "the better part". He thinks that the first duty of man is to achieve the kingdom of God in his own soul and that, in order to attain such an end, the best way is to stand face to face with God in silence and retreat. Therefore the religious life means to him the life of primitive monasticism. These primeval forms have survived in the East more than in the West. One could still find stylites in Russia in the sixteenth century. The most ancient forms of solitary life may still be found to-day on Mount Athos. St. Seraphim of Sarov, during the first third of the nineteenth century, spent years of seclusion in a cell or on stone amidst the forest. The mantle of Elijah has fallen on many Elishas.

(5) The liturgical element

Orthodox piety is liturgical in many ways. First, the Orthodox Church dispenses not only the Word, but the Sacraments. Second, the liturgical worship of the Orthodox Church is extremely elaborate, full of spiritual meaning and beauty. Thirdly, collective forms of worship predominate over "private devotions". Lastly, the Church calendar frames the whole year in the stages of the Saviour's earthly life.

But, besides the general setting and inspiration which the Church's ritual gives to the religious life, there exists, within the Orthodox tradition, a properly "liturgical" line of thought and piety. A whole school of saints and doctors have conceived the entire Christian life according to a liturgical type and rhythm ; it is in the Church ritual that they seek and find the successive stages of the normal development of the Christian soul.

We cannot avoid facing the very difficult question of a possible influence of the "mystery cults" on Hellenistic Christianity. That the Eleusinian and other mysteries were the origin of Christianity we do not admit. That Christianity sometimes borrowed from the vocabulary and rites of the "mystery-cults" does not seem impossible. The Greek Church, as was natural, may have been instrumental in an adjustment which does not mean a corruption of the truth. Why not admit, as a parallel to the Jewish *praeparatio evangelica*, another *praeparatio evangelica* represented by some "mysteric" aspects of Hellenism ?

Another factor in the growth of Orthodox ritualism was undoubtedly the influence of the ceremonial of the Byzantine Court. But, whatever this influence may have been, it remains true that the essentials of the Orthodox rites have a Scriptural origin. At the bottom of all these ritual developments, however complex they may be, we find certain very simple elements drawn from the Old and New Testaments, such as baptism by water, unction with oil, the laying-on of hands, the breaking of bread.

The "mystagogical (or liturgical) theology" in the Orthodox Church had many famous exponents. St. Cyril of Jerusalem (fourth century) and Theodore of Mopsuesta wrote Catecheses which expound the Christian life on the basis of the holy mysteries.[1]

The *Celestial Hierarchy* of the pseudo-Dionysius and the *Mystagogy* of St. Maximus the Confessor contain much more speculation and symbolism and have exercised a larger influence, but do not go deeper. St. Germanus, Patriarch of Constantinople (729), has been considered—wrongly, as it seems—to be the author of an *Ecclesiastical History and Mystical Contemplation* which, in fact, is a commentary on

[1] *P.G.* XXXIII, 1066–1127 and LXVI, 73.

the three eucharistic liturgies in use within the Orthodox Church.[1] Simeon of Thessalonica wrote a treatise *On the divine Temple*.[2]

But the greatest of the liturgical theologians of the Orthodox Church undoubtedly is Nicholas Cabasilas (*c.* 1371), often confused with Nilus Cabasilas, bishop of Salonica, and with the courtier Cabasilas the Sakellarios. Nicholas Cabasilas wrote an *Interpretation of the Divine Liturgy*.[3] His chief work was *Life in Christ*.[1] This work,[4] in seven books, is an analysis of the sacraments and also of the rites of the consecration of the altar. Cabasilas has nothing of the exclusive or narrow ritualist about him. He is anxious to link liturgical piety with Christology and asceticism. He recommends meditation and mental prayer as the safest way to bind us to Christ. He says in penetrating accents : "The one pattern is Jesus. . . . The Saviour is more intimate to us than our own soul. . . . We are concorporeal with Him, living His life, and have become His members." The person of Jesus, according to him, is the heart of the Mystical Body of Christ. Cabasilas' works were consulted as witnesses to the tradition during the deliberations of the Council of Trent. Bossuet called him "one of the most solid theologians of the Greek Church". The late Jesuit theologian, M. de la Taille, often quotes him in his admirable *Mysterium fidei* (1921).

In recent times the *Sacred Catechesis* (1683) of the Greek Nicholas Bulgaris (*c.* 1684), the *Consideration on the Divine Liturgy* of Gogol, and the collection of Slavonic liturgical books translated into German and commented upon by the Russian priest A. Maltzev, belong to the "mystagogical" tradition.

One of the aspects of liturgical piety is the veneration paid to ikons and relics, the worship (*douleia*, "service",

---

[1] *P.G.* XCVIII, 384–454.
[2] *P.G.* CL. 387–491.
[3] *P.G.* CLV, 732–733.
[4] *P.G.* C.L., 493–725.

timē, *sebasmos*, and not *latreia* or adoration, due to God only) of saints, which began with the commemoration of the death (*dies natalis*) of martyrs. Marian piety has developed in the Greek Church mainly through the writings of St. Andrew of Crete (eighth century), St. John Damascene (eighth century), and St. Sergius of Constantinople (*c.* 638).

(6) *The contemplative element*

Finally we must consider a factor of Orthodox spirituality which we would call the properly "contemplative" element, i.e. the tradition of the specialists and technicians of contemplation.

The pseudo-Dionysius coined the term "mystical theology" and evolved a theory of contemplation. But it was in the course of the Byzantine Middle Ages that contemplation developed within the Orthodox Church as a special discipline and technique. This is mainly due to the movement called Hesychasm.

The tradition of the "hesychasts" (*hesychia*, "quiet") goes back to a very great mystic, St. Symeon the New Theologian (949–1022), higumen (abbot) of St. Mamas of Xylokerkos, author of the *Hymns of divine love*, and to his disciple Nicetas Stēthatos (*c.* 1050). Mount Athos afterwards became the centre of Hesychasm. During the fourteenth century, Hesychasm was identified with the theories of St. Gregory Palamas, Archbishop of Salonica, on the "uncreated light", conceptions disputed by Barlaam and Gregory the Sinaite. In order to understand and estimate Hesychasm, it is advisable to disentangle it from the violent polemics which "Palamism" has raised and which interest dogmatic theology more than spirituality.

Four main points seem to us characteristic of the hesychast method :

(1) the striving towards a state of total rest or quiet, which excludes reading, psalmody, meditation, etc. ;

(2) the repetition of the "Jesus-prayer" ;

(3) practices designed to help the concentration of the mind, such as physical immobility, control or suspension of breathing, fixation of the eyes on the heart, the stomach and the navel, in order to "let the mind go back into the heart" ; this last operation was called *omphaloscopia* or *omphalopsychia* ;

(4) the feeling of an inner warmth and physical perception of a "divine light" or "light of Tabor".

Points (2) and (3) are not in contradiction with point (1). They are parts of the general striving indicated in (1) ; they afford the means which prepare and produce the state of quiet. This state culminates with the luminous perception described in point (4). At such a state prayer is not non-existent, but latent and quiescent in the soul.

This scheme of contemplation calls for a few remarks. In the first place the hesychasts never dreamt of proposing an infallible technique. They do not offer "recipes", able automatically to bring man to contemplation. They do not sever their contemplative disciplines from ascetism, purity of heart and charity. The inner endeavour to come nearer to God remains foremost.

Such an exercise as *omphaloscopia* may seem to us a strange practice, more akin to *yoga* than to the Gospel. But St. Ignatius Loyola himself did not hesitate to give in his Exercises very precise directions about bodily attitudes and material surroundings during meditation. Vladimir Soloviev, too, recommended the control of breathing as an aid to prayer. All these things have but a very secondary importance. The only question is whether, in given cases, they may prove helpful and facilitate what is essential.

As to the perception of a divine light (leaving aside the question of the exact nature of that light), here we find again a classical experience of the Christian mystics and, before them, of the Jewish mystics (the "glory of God" as a luminous appearance, *shekinah*, *kabod*, *doxa*). But again this accessory phenomenon must not be mistaken for the essentials, which are of an inner and invisible order.

Shortly before 1914 the question of the "Jesus-prayer" raised a new controversy on Mount Athos. A mystical school extolled the worship of the Sacred Name of Jesus (*onomatolatreia*) as of the actual bearer of Divinity. This is patently unacceptable. But that a kind of sacramental value attaches to the Name of Jesus should not be ruled out. As a matter of fact, such a sacramental view of the Name of our Lord (using the word "sacramental" in a wide sense) is quite in conformity with the general mind of the Orthodox Church. The "Jesus-prayer" has been intensively in use during the last twenty years, mainly, it seems, among the Russian emigration, and independently of any special theory about the Sacred Name. Here is one of the most living and interesting aspects of Orthodox mysticism.

When we speak of Hesychasm, we must be careful to assign to each element its right proportions, and first to Hesychasm itself. Hesychasm in the Orthodox Church may be compared with the great Spanish school of mystics in the Latin Church of the sixteenth century. In both cases we find a remarkable endeavour to simplify and systematize the spiritual ways, to make them more practical and accessible. But St. Theresa, St. John of the Cross, and St. Ignatius Loyola do not surpass and still less supersede St. Augustine, St. Benedict, St. Gregory the Great, St. Bernard and St. Thomas. In the same way Symeon the New Theologian, Nicetas Stethatos, and Gregory Palamas neither surpass nor supersede St. Basil, St. Chrysostom, St. Gregory of Nazianzus and St. Gregory of Nyssa—the Fathers and most authorized interpreters, not only of Orthodox thought but of Orthodox piety as well. And beyond the contemplative mystics, beyond the Fathers themselves, the simple and pure Gospel remains central.

CHAPTER II

THE ESSENTIALS OF ORTHODOX SPIRITUALITY

WE HAVE SEEN the successive growths which have, in the course of history, shaped the spirituality of the Orthodox Church. We shall now try to extricate what is common to these various elements and thus, delving beyond accidental diversities of attitude and expression, reach the essential foundations of Orthodox spirituality.

(1) *Aim and means of Christian life*

The aim of man's life is union (*henōsis*) with God and deification (*theōsis*).

The Greek Fathers have used the term "deification" to a greater extent than the Latins. What is meant is not, of course, a pantheistic identity, but a sharing, through grace, in the divine life : ". . . Whereby are given unto us exceeding great and precious promises : that by these ye might be partakers of the divine nature . . ." (2 Pet. 1. 4).

This participation takes man within the life of the three Divine Persons themselves, in the incessant circulation and overflowing of love which courses between the Father, the Son and the Spirit, and which expresses the very nature of God. Here is the true and eternal bliss of man.

Union with God is the perfect fulfilment of the "kingdom" announced by the Gospel, and of that charity or love which sums up all the Law and the Prophets. Only in union with the life of the Three Persons is man enabled to love God with his whole heart, soul and mind, and his neighbour as himself.

Union between God and Man cannot be achieved without a Mediator, who is the Word made Flesh, our Lord Jesus

Christ : "I am the Way . . . no man cometh unto the Father but by Me" (John 14. 6).

In the Son we become sons. "We are made sons of God" says St. Athanasius.[1]   Incorporation into Christ is the only means to reach our supernatural end.

The Holy Ghost operates and perfects this incorporation. St. Irenaeus writes : "Through the Spirit one ascends to the Son and through the Son to the Father." [2]

The fact that the object of Christian spirituality is the *supernatural* life of the soul and not the natural effects, either normal or supernormal, obtained by human disciplines, even when they are called "religious", cannot be over-emphasized. What is here in question is the action of God on the soul, and not the human actions on the soul itself. The basis of spiritual life is not psychological, but onto-logical. Therefore an accurate treatise on spirituality is not the description of certain states of the soul, mystical or otherwise, but the objective application of definite theo-logical principles to the individual soul. The redeeming action of our Lord constitutes the alpha and omega as well as the centre of Christian spirituality.

(2) *Divine grace and human will*

The incorporation of man into Christ and his union with God require the co-operation of two unequal, but equally necessary, forces : divine grace and human will.

Will—and not intellect or feeling—is the chief human instrument of the union with God. There can be no intimate union with God if our own will is not surrendered and conformed to the divine will, "Sacrifice and offering Thou wouldest not. . . . Lo, I come to do Thy Will, O God " (Heb. 10. 5, 9).

But our weak human will remains powerless if it is not anticipated and upheld by the grace of God. "Through the

[1] II *Contra Arianos*, XLIII.   [2] *Adv. Haeres*. V. 36. 2.

grace of the Lord Jesus we shall be saved" (Acts 15. 11).
It is grace that achieves in us both the willing and the doing.

The Christian East did not experience the controversies
which raged in the West around the notions of grace and
predestination (Augustinianism, Pelagianism and semi-Pela-
gianism, Thomism, Calvinism, Jansenism, Molinism). In
the Orthodox Church the idea of grace has kept something
of the vernal freshness which the word *charis* evoked to the
Greek minds : an idea of luminous beauty, free gift, condescension and harmony.

The Greek Fathers emphasized human freedom in the
work of salvation. This emphasis strikingly contrasts with
St. Augustine's language. St. John Chrysostom writes :
"We must first select good, and then God adds what
appertains to His office ; He does not act antecedently to
our will, so as not to destroy our liberty." [1] These words
have almost a semi-Pelagian flavour. We ought to remember that the Greek Fathers had not to deal with the Pelagian
heresy. On the contrary, their fight was directed against
an oriental fatalist gnosis. Chrysostom fully acknowledged antecedent grace and its necessity. He writes elsewhere : "You do not hold of yourself, but you have received
from God. Hence you have received what you possess, and
not only this or that, but everything you have. For these
are not your own merits, but the grace of God. Although
you cite faith, you owe it nevertheless to call." [2] Origen
had already taught that grace reinforces voluntary energy
without destroying freedom. St. Ephraim wrote on the
necessity of the divine help.

Clement of Alexandria coined the word "synergy" (co-
operation) in order to express the action of these two con-
joined energies : grace and human will. The term and idea
of synergy have remained and represent, until to-day, the
doctrine of the Orthodox Church on these matters.

[1] *Hom. XII in Hebr.*   [2] *Hom. XII in 1 Cor.*

(3) *Asceticism and Mysticism*

Both the distinction between the human will and divine grace, and their interpenetration, help us to understand how, in the spiritual life, the ascetical and mystical elements can differ and mingle.

Asceticism is generally understood as an "exercise" of human will on itself, in order to improve itself. As to the term "mysticism," modern language has sadly misused it. "Mystical" is confused with "obscure," "poetic," "irrational," etc. Not only unbelieving psychologists, like Delacroix and Janet, but Christian writers, such as von Hügel, and Evelyn Underhill, exhibit a lack of precision in their conception of mysticism. To define it as an experimental knowledge of divine things gets near the truth, but still remains too vague. The masters of the spiritual life and, following them, recent Roman writers (Garrigou-Lagrange, de Guibert, Maritain) have had the merit of giving precision to this terminology. They give to the words "ascetical" and "mystical" a very strict technical meaning. The "ascetical life" is a life in which "acquired" virtues, i.e. virtues resulting from a personal effort, only accompanied by that general grace which God grants to every good will, prevail. The "mystical life" is a life in which the gifts of the Holy Spirit are predominant over human efforts, and in which "infused" virtues are predominant over the "acquired" ones ; the soul has become more passive than active.

Let us use a classical comparison. Between the ascetic life, that is, the life in which human action predominates, and the mystical life, that is, the life in which God's action predominates, there is the same difference as between rowing a boat and sailing it ; the oar is the ascetic effort, the sail is the mystical passivity which is unfurled to catch the divine wind.

This view of asceticism and mysticism is excellent. It coincides perfectly with the theology of the Greek Fathers.

These do not give technical definitions of asceticism and mysticism, but they distinguish very sharply between the state in which man is "acting" and the state in which he is "acted upon". The pseudo-Dionysius remarks that divine love tends to ecstasy (*ecstatikos ho theios erōs*), i.e. conduces to a state in which man is taken out of himself and his normal condition.

One must be careful, however, not to raise a wall of separation between mystical and ascetic life. The prevalence of the gifts does not exclude the practice of acquired virtues, any more than the prevalence of acquired virtues excludes the gifts. One of these two elements, of course, predominates over the other. But the spiritual life is generally a synthesis of the "ascetical" and the "mystical."

To the mystical life belong the charisms and the extraordinary phenomena which accompany certain states of prayer : inner locutions, visions—stigmatization seems to be a property of the West. Neither these phenomena nor the charisms constitute the essence of the mystic life. However great may be their significance, they are only accidents. Mystical life consists in the supreme reign of the gifts of the Holy Spirit over the soul.

Graces of the mystic order are not necessary to salvation. Mystical life is not synonymous with Christian perfection : this last consists in charity or love, and may be reached by souls who will never know any other way than the simple and loving keeping of the commandments. But most of the Greek Fathers, with their sanctified optimism, seem to favour the thesis nowadays defended by the Dominicans and Maritain : that the mystical graces, far from being the privilege of a few elect, are offered to all souls of good will. Their empirical rareness comes from the fact that not many people answer the call. They are nevertheless the normal—though not necessary—blossoming of a genuine Christian life. The King wishes that all should sit at the table of the Messianic feast. Our Lord came to kindle a fire upon earth ; what does He wish but to see this living flame burning in everyone ?

(4) *Prayer and Contemplation*

Prayer is a necessary instrument of salvation. Cassian, whose voice is the echo of the Desert Fathers, distinguishes three ascending degrees of the Christian prayer : supplication (for oneself), intercession (for others), thanksgiving or praise. These three degrees of prayer constitute in themselves a whole programme of spiritual life. It matters little whether prayer is vocal or mental ; the most loving prayer, either vocal or mental, is always the best.

In contrast with prayer, contemplation is not necessary to salvation. But, as a general rule, assiduous and fervent prayer becomes contemplative.

What is contemplation ? [1] It is not synonymous with high intellectual speculations or extraordinary insight, which are the property of certain rare and chosen souls. According to the "classics" of the spiritual life, contemplation begins with the "prayer of simplicity" or "prayer of simple regard". The prayer of simplicity consists in placing yourself in the presence of God and maintaining yourself in His presence for a certain time, in an interior silence which is as complete as possible, while you concentrate upon the divine Object, reduce to unity the multiplicity of your thought and feelings, and endeavour to "keep yourself quiet" without words or arguments. This prayer of simplicity is the frontier and the most elementary degree of contemplation. It is not difficult. Anyone who is even to a slight degree accustomed to pray is sure to have experienced this form of contemplation, for a few minutes at least. It is marvel-

[1] In the course of this chapter we reproduce, with the leave of the editor of *Sobornost*, some passages from an article published by us, under the title "On Contemplation" in *Sobornost* of June, 1941.

lously fruitful.   It is like a welcome shower of rain falling on
the garden of the soul.   It gives most powerful assistance
to the efforts which we make in the moral order to avoid sin
and to accomplish the divine will.

It is good to make acts of contemplation.   But to live a
contemplative life is better still.   We must not imagine
that the contemplative life means a life in which one does
nothing but contemplate.   Were that so, the contemplative
life would be possible only in the desert or the cloister, while
it is, as a matter of fact, open to all.   The contemplative
life is simply a life orientated towards contemplation, a life
arranged in such a way that acts of contemplation are fairly
often possible in it and form its summit.   If each day you
give some moments to the prayer of simplicity; if you know
how to separate yourself interiorly, in some degree, from
persons and things in order to enter into yourself, and not
allow yourself to be dominated by them; if, in your thinking and reading, you bring with you a certain preoccupa-
tion with God and attentiveness to His presence; you are
already beginning to lead the contemplative life, even if you
are still in the world.

Contemplation is *acquired* if the acts of contemplation are
the results of personal effort.   It is *infused* if these acts are
produced by divine grace without, or almost without,
human effort.   Acquired contemplation belongs to the
ascetical life.   Infused contemplation belongs to the
mystical life.   This last is the normal culmination of the
contemplative life.

There is a correspondence between classification of the
stages of contemplation in the West and their classification
in the East.   St. Theresa established the classification
of the states of contemplative prayer prevalent in the West.
She distinguished four aspects of it : (1) the prayer of quiet,
silent concentration of the soul on God, which however does
not exclude distractions ; (2) full union, in which there are

no longer distractions, and which is accompanied by a feeling of "ligature of the powers" of the soul ; (3) ecstatic union, in which the soul "goes out of itself"; (4) transforming union, or spiritual marriage. We find in the Greek Fathers, if not such a precise classification as St. Theresa's, at least certain parallel distinctions. The prayer of simple regard, the prayer of quiet, and the full union are degrees of the *hesychia*, which is, in some form or other, the introduction to Eastern contemplation. Above the *hesychia* comes the ecstatic union, of which instances are found in the New Testament and which is described exactly by the Fathers of the Desert and the pseudo-Dionysius (in their theory of the *ekstasis* and of the circular movement, *kyklike kinēsis*, bringing the soul back to God). The transforming union or spiritual marriage are described both by those who conceive spiritual life as a deification (*theōsis*) and by those who lay stress on the nuptial relationship between the soul and her Lord (Origen, Methodius of Olympus). An imperceptible transition, an unbroken chain of intermediate shades, links these states one to the other. Thus it happens, in Orthodox practice, that the Name of Jesus (which is really the heart and the strength of the "Jesus-prayer") may be used, not only as the starting point, but also in continuous support of mystical states ranging from *hesychia* to *ekstasis*.

What has been said about the mystical life must be repeated about the contemplative life. They are not the privilege of certain exceptional souls. It is indeed true that monasticism offers specially favourable conditions for the practice of contemplation. Nevertheless, contemplation is open to all. Marriage, family life, a profession or a trade in no way exclude contemplative prayer and mystical graces. On the contrary, the contemplative or the mystic is a very special source of blessing for the medium in which he lives (though this will frequently not prevent that medium from causing him to suffer). Leaving aside some of the more elevated mystical states, such as ecstasy and the spiritual marriage, we hold that the prayer of simplicity and the mystical stages that follow it, namely, the prayer of quiet and the non-ecstatic prayer of union—we would, according to the Eastern terminology, say, rather, the initial hesychast states —are the normal end of any habitual and loving prayer-life that has as its object the keeping of the Saviour's precepts, and is accompanied by faithfulness to them. Contemplation is often the best means of becoming faithful to those precepts. For contemplation increases love, and love makes us able to keep the commandments : we can pass from love to the keeping of the commandments, but the converse is hardly possible.

Again and again it must be said that contemplation, no more than mysticism, should be identified with perfection—which is charity (love). But a contemplation which would be the utmost exercise of charity, *culmen caritatis*, would also be the acme of perfection, *culmen perfectionis*. Such a contemplation would constitute an end to which it would indeed be worth subordinating all human life.

(5) *The Holy Mysteries*

The Orthodox Church calls *mysterion* (mystery) what the Latin Church calls *sacramentum*. The holy mysteries are neither the end nor yet the essence of spiritual life. They are means of grace, and only means. But these means have, in the life of the Orthodox Church, an importance which must be exactly understood and measured.

One might call the Orthodox Church a "mysteric" Church in several senses.

First, the Orthodox Church adopts, in regard to the sacraments, a realist attitude. She believes that the sacraments are not mere symbols of divine things, but that the gift of a spiritual reality is attached to the sign perceptible by the senses. She believes that, in these mysteries, the same graces are present nowadays which were formerly imparted in the Upper Room, or at the waters where the disciples of Jesus baptized, or in the declarations of forgiveness that sinners received from our Lord, or in the descent of the Dove, and so on. In each of those divine gifts there is a mystical as well as an ascetical aspect. The mystical aspect consists in the fact that sacramental grace is not the outcome of human efforts, but is objectively bestowed by our Lord. The ascetical aspect consists in the fact that the holy mysteries bring forth their fruit in the soul of the grown-up recipient only if that soul is assenting to, and prepared for, it.

The Orthodox Church is also "mysteric" in another way. She is somewhat reticent concerning her intimate treasures. She keeps in the word "mysterion" its meaning of "secret". She fears familiarity. She veils and covers what the Latin Church lays open and exhibits. She feels reluctant to regulate the approach to the holy mysteries by precise disciplinary canons and to utter too detailed statements on the nature of such or such a mystery (e.g. on the Eucharistic Presence). She avoids giving officially too many strict definitions. This indefiniteness has a very simple explanation. The Orthodox Church wants a mystery to remain a "mystery", and not to become a theorem, or a juridical institution. For the Orthodox Church is not only "mysteric", but "pneumatic", and the *Mysterion* is conditioned by the *Pneuma*, the Spirit.

There is "one greater than the Temple" (Matt. 12. 6), and greater than the Holy Mysteries. The scholastic axiom *Deus non alligatur sacramentis*—"God is not bound to the sacraments"—may have a Western origin, but expresses quite well the Eastern mind. What Orthodox would dare to assert that the members of the Society of Friends are deprived of the graces that the sacraments represent? The angel went down at regular times into the pool, and whosoever stepped in first after the troubling of

the waters was made whole ; but our Lord directly healed the
paralytic who could not step in (John 5). This does not mean
that a man could disregard, or slight, or despise, the channels
of grace offered by the Church without endangering his soul.
It means that no externals, however useful, are *necessary to
God*, in the absolute sense of this word, and that there is no
institution, however sacred, which God cannot dispense with.

Nothing that could be called a sacramental materialism
will be found among the Greek Fathers. They remind us
that to keep God's Word is quite as important as to approach
the Holy Mysteries. Origen, speaking of the precautions
surrounding the Eucharist, writes : "Now, if you exercise
so much caution when guarding His body, and rightly, how
is it that you consider it a lesser fault to have neglected the
Word of God than His Body ? " [1]

(6) *The Communion of Saints*

In a vision of the *Shepherd*, Hermas saw Rhoda whom he
had loved and who, affectionately reproaching him and also
smilingly comforting him, manifested to him, from heaven,
that she was helping him by the Lord. This second-century
vision shows what is the Communion of Saints (*Koinōnia
tōn hagiōn*)—a sharing of the prayers and good works of the
heavenly and earthly Christians and a familiar intercourse
between ourselves and the glorified saints. The spiritual
life of an Orthodox would not be complete without this
brotherly relationship.

As we have already indicated, the worship of the saints is
not *latreia*, the adoration due to God, but *douleia*, service or
sebasmos, veneration. It is also called *proskynesis timetike*,
i.e. the veneration "paid to all that is endowed with some
dignity," as St. John Damascene soberly says.[2] But our
relationship with the saints implies more than certain marks
of honour. Just as a living Christian can beg the interces-

[1] *In Exod. Hom.* XIII, 3.   [2] *Orat.* III, 40.

sion of another living Christian, so we commend ourselves to the prayers of the Saints.

Among the Saints, the Apostles and the Martyrs hold an eminent place according to primitive Christian tradition. The Orthodox Church prepares by a special Lent for the feast of the Holy Apostles Peter and Paul, St. Gregory Nazianzen had a special devotion to St. Cyprian, St. Basil towards St. Mammas, St. Gregory of Nyssa towards St. Theodore. St. Ephraim writes : "Remember, O Lord, the tears I have shed before Thy holy martyrs." The Orthodox Church gives a great place in her calendar to the patriarchs, prophets, and just men of the Old Testament, contrary to the practice of the Latin Church. High above all are the Angels, classified into hierarchies by the pseudo-Dionysius. The detail of the classification matters little, but its underlying ideas are agreeable to Scripture. The Greek Fathers laid a particular stress on guardian angels. Origen already taught their existence. The pseudo-Dionysius said that they not only watch over us, but convey to us light and perfect us. Chrysostom called his guardian angel his "pedagogue", Basil and Cyril of Alexandria called theirs "fellow wayfarer" and "preceptor" respectively. There are local angels. Gregory Nazienzen prayed, in a moving way, to the angel protectors of Constantinople.[1] Bishop Theophane the Recluse advises "listening to the thoughts which come during prayer, especially in the morning", which he ascribes to the influence of a guardian angel.

Bulgakov has built up interesting theories about the guardian angels ; he sees in them something like the "idea" (in the Platonic sense) and the "pattern" of each man. But we may abide in the Biblical conception according to which angels are more than the bearers of divine messages and the guides of men : they are bearers of the very Name and Power of God. There is nothing rosy or weakly poetical in the

[1] *Orat.* 42, *P.G.* IX, 36, 459.

Angels of the Bible: they are flashes of the light and strength of the Almighty Lord. The early Christians—and the Eastern saints perhaps more than the Western—had visions and dreams of angels. An integral Christian life should imply a daily and familiar intercourse with the angelic world. The experiences of Jacob should become ours: "And Jacob went on his way, and the angels of God met him. . . . And there wrestled a man with him until the breaking of the day. . . . And he said: I will not let thee go, except thou bless me. . . . And he dreamed, and, behold, a ladder set up on the earth, and the top of it reached to heaven: and behold the angels of God ascending and descending on it" (Gen. 32. 1, 24, 26, and 28. 12).

At the summit of the celestial hierarchy is the *Theotokos*, the blessed Virgin Mary and Mother of God incarnate, whom the Orthodox Church, chiefly since the Council of Ephesus (431), has surrounded with a worship exceeding that of the other saints. A special Lent and numerous feasts and hymns are dedicated to her. Since the Gospel is the first and main source of Orthodox piety, the most Orthodox form of piety towards the Mother of the Saviour is undoubtedly the "evangelical" one, i.e. piety towards Mary as it flows from the sacred texts themselves. Four passages seem to us specially important. First, the angelic salutation: "Hail, thou that art highly favoured, the Lord is with thee: blessed art thou among women," and Mary's answer: "Behold the handmaid of the Lord; be it unto according to thy word" (Luke 1. 28, 38). Secondly, the attitude of Mary at the marriage in Cana of Galilee: "The mother of Jesus saith unto Him, They have no wine . . . His mother saith unto the servants: Whatsoever He saith unto you, do it" (John 2. 3, 5). Thirdly, the short dialogue between a certain woman and our Lord: "Blessed is the womb that bare Thee. . . . But He said, Yea, rather, blessed are they that hear the word of God and keep it" (Luke 11.

27, 28)—a declaration which does not disparage Mary, but points out where her true merit lies. And finally, the words of Jesus on the Cross : "He saith unto His mother, Woman, behold thy son. Then saith He to the disciple : Behold thy mother," with the practical conclusion : "And from that hour that disciple took her unto his own home" (John 19. 26, 27). These texts are the roots of true Marian piety.

We must say here a few words about the ikons which occupy such a place in the life of prayer of the Orthodox, chiefly since the defeat of iconoclasm and the institution of the Feast of Orthodoxy (11th March, 843). Let us first notice that the Eastern ikon is not, like the Latin image (either painted or sculptured), a resemblance. The Orthodox Church keeps the precept of the Decalogue : "Thou shalt not make unto thee any graven image or likeness . . ." (Exod. 20. 4). The ikon is a kind of hieroglyph, a stylized symbol, a sign, an abstract scheme. The more an ikon tends to reproduce human features, the more it swerves from the iconographical canons admitted by the Church. Far from being the manifestation of a religious sensualism or materialism, the Orthodox conception of the ikon expresses an almost puritanical hostility against the "sensuous". Some recent Orthodox writers (Bulgakov, Ostrogorsky) see another difference between the ikon and the Latin image or statue. While the likeness is for the West a means of evocation and teaching, the Eastern ikon is a means of communion. The ikon is loaded with the grace of an objective presence ; it is a meeting place between the believer and the Heavenly World. This is taught by St. Theodore the Studite, and also in certain Greek texts of the ninth century which set the ikon side by side with the Eucharist.[1] But the official documents of the Orthodox Church adopt a somewhat cooler view, which entirely coincides with the attitude of the Latin Church. The

[1] See *Roma e l'Oriente*, V, p. 351.

Second Council of Nicaea says : "We paint them (the saints) because we would have their virtues to imitate, and we retrace their lives in books . . . for our benefit." The same Council of 787 says again : "The honour paid to the image goes over to the pretotype." St. John Damascene compares the ikon to the word or the book : it is a memorial, *hypomnema*. Let us add that ikon-worship, which could not be attacked without heresy, is not as a practice binding on any individual.

As there is an "evangelical piety" towards Mary, there is also an "evangelical piety" towards the saints, and we shall repeat that the most evangelical is always the most Orthodox. The evangelical attitude towards the saints is indicated in John 12. 20–22 : "And there were certain Greeks . . . that came up to worship at the feast. The same came therefore to Philip . . . saying : Sir, we would see Jesus. Philip cometh and telleth Andrew ; and again Andrew and Philip tell Jesus." And in Luke 22. 11 : "The Master saith unto thee, Where is the guestchamber where I shall eat the passover with my disciples ?"

(7) *The stages of the spiritual life*

The attempt was made very early to distinguish ascending stages in the spiritual life. The distinction between the three ways—purgative, illuminative, unitive—has become classical in the West. Its origin is Eastern : it is due to the pseudo-Dionysius. St. Basil and Cassian discriminate between beginners, proficients and the perfect. The Alexandrines and Diodore of Photike mention three types of Christians: the *eisagogikos*, "introduced" or "approaching", who is mainly concerned with the practice of virtues (*praxis*) ; then the *mesos* or "middle one", to whom contemplation (*theoria*) and the suppression of passions (*apatheia*) are particularly suitable ; at last the *teleios*, "perfect", who is qualified for the true experimental knowledge of God (*theologia*).

Under different names these classifications generally recur, and they contain a nucleus of truth. But none has an absolute value. The various states penetrate each other. The soul rises and falls back from one to the other without following any rule. Moreover these classifications express states of the soul rather than the objective data of God's action. They mark some moments of our own human existence rather than moments of the life of our Saviour. They are anthropocentric rather than theocentric. Finally they represent the interesting views of eminent spiritual writers, but they lack the authority of the Church.

Hence the question : would it be possible to discover an itinerary of spiritual life officially proposed by the Church and emphasizing the divine operation rather than the psychology of the soul *in via* ?

Nicholas Cabasilas shows us where the scale of the degrees of sanctification adopted by the Orthodox Church is to be found. He distinguishes three essential moments in spiritual life : Baptism, Chrisma (confirmation by unction), Eucharist. This is not a private view. The official spirituality of the Orthodox Church is consigned in her text-book of sanctification, that is, in the Ritual (Greek *Euchologion*, Slavonic *Trebnik*). The Ritual takes man from his baptism and accompanies him to his burial ; it constitutes the most authoritative treatise on the spiritual life. The order in which it presents the holy mysteries expresses the ascending order of the sanctification of the soul according to the mind and intention of the Church.

Therefore one might say that the three holy mysteries of Baptism, Chrisma and Eucharist are the three essential stages in the way that leads to God. The other sacraments and sacramentals may be connected with one or another of these three degrees and mysteries. Penance, the first monastic profession, the second wedding and the unction of the sick are connected with Baptism. The first wedding, the great monastic profession and ordination are connected with the Eucharist. Ordinations and the anointing of Kings (in the Byzantine tradition) are also connected with Chrisma. We shall come back to these points.

Not only the sacraments, or solemn rites respected almost as sacraments, but all the aspects of the life of prayer of the Church, her feasts, her calendar, her hymns, are focussed in these three mysteries. The Holy Liturgy in the strict sense, i.e. the Lord's Supper, sums up their meaning. The first part of our Eucharistic Liturgy is called the Liturgy of the Catechumens, because the candidates for Baptism were allowed to be present. The part of the liturgy called *anaphora*, which culminates in the *epiklesis* or invocation of the Holy Ghost on the Eucharistic Gifts, is particularly linked with Chrisma as sacrament of the Spirit. The part of the Liturgy constituted by the communion is the Eucharist itself, the meal of the immolated Body and Blood of the Lord Jesus.

Does this mean that our whole spiritual life is merely a ritual life ? Chiefly in this field we must guard ourselves against a deadly literalism : "It is the spirit that quickeneth ; the flesh profiteth nothing : the words that I speak unto you, they are spirit, and they are life" (John 6. 63). We must go beyond the letter, beyond the mere visible celebration of the three sacraments of Baptism, Chrisma and Eucharist, and perceive the invisible graces which they express. Baptism, Chrisma and the Lord's Supper are *signa*, signs. Baptismal grace, Pentecostal grace, Paschal grace are *res*, the realities behind the signs. The signs, is it true, confer the realities, but the realities overflow the signs. It is the realities that matter and that we must strain after. These three graces are given with the corresponding holy mysteries, and are in some way supported by them. The Lord can nevertheless impart them to souls which never receive the sacramental signs. He can also revive them (as in the case of perfect contrition) within souls which received the grace with the sacrament and then lost it, and this revivification is not necessarily accompanied by the performance of sacramental rites. Baptismal grace, Pentecostal grace, and Paschal grace exist wherever supernatural love exists. They are the very texture of spiritual life.

In the Church Ritual, the Chrisma precedes the Eucharist. It will be objected that Pentecostal grace was given to the Apostles after Paschal grace. This is true only in appearance. At the time of the first Easter the Apostles obtained only an incomplete experience of Paschal grace : they shared in the Lord's Supper and in the joy of the Presence of the Risen Lord, but they did not share in the immolation of Christ. They knew the fullness of Paschal grace only at the end of their life, when their own martyrdom joined with Christ's sacrifice. Pentecost was for them the necessary condition of this full Paschal grace, just as the gift of the Spirit is for us the necessary condition of a full eucharistic life.

The three graces—Baptismal grace, Pentecostal grace, Paschal grace—are but aspects of one and the same divine grace. They can never be kept asunder; they almost coexist. When we say that, in the mind of the Church, they represent an ascending order, we mean that in the course of the normal and untroubled growth of a soul, each of these aspects should predominate in its turn and in its own time.

Symbolically, we could imagine these three theological graces as the *Charites* of ancient Hellas—the three chaste, generous and beautiful maidens who formed an interwoven group, *manibus amplexis*, says Seneca. Or we can think of them as of a cantata for three voices. Each voice dominates in its turn, but the other two never cease to accompany the dominant one. Or again, if we turned to the representations of primitive · Christian art, we could say that Baptismal grace finds its expression in the Ichthys, the divine Fish ; Pentecostal grace in the descent of the Dove ; Paschal grace in the immolation and triumph of the Lamb.

But let us, rather, leave these images aside. We shall go deeper if we understand that these three graces express three moments in the life of our Lord : His own contact with the baptismal waters ; His reception and sending of the Paraclete ; and finally His Passover. Our own spiritual experiences are but weak reflections of His life. The baptizing Christ (who is also the forgiving and healing Christ), Christ the sender of the Spirit, and Christ the Paschal Lamb, or, rather, our true Passover : such are the aspects of our Lord, the revelation and inner experience of which constitute the spiritual life of the Christian. Let us examine each of them in greater detail.

CHAPTER III

THE BAPTIZING CHRIST

(1) *Jesus and the Water of Life*

ONE OF THE favourite themes of primitive Christian art is Moses striking the rock with his rod and causing water to gush out. The water-theme comes over and over again in the Old Testament, from the crossing of the Red Sea by Israel, to Isaiah's call : "Ho, every one that thirsteth, come ye to the waters . . ." (Isa. 55. 1). The fulfilment of these passages of Scripture is to be found in the words of Our Lord reported in the Gospel : "Except a man be born of Water and of the Spirit, he cannot enter into the Kingdom of God (John 3. 5) ; if any man thirst, let him come unto me and drink. He that believeth on me . . . out of his belly shall flow rivers of living water" (John 7. 37, 38).

Water has become the sign of salvation. Our Lord commanded His disciples to baptize : "Go ye therefore, and teach all the nations, baptizing them . . ." (Matt. 28. 19). He Himself inaugurated His public ministry by receiving the baptism of John. Eastern Fathers, chiefly St. Ignatius of Antioch, teach that the contact of our Lord's body with the water of Jordan is the principle of the sanctifying action of water in the holy mystery of Baptism.[1]

The Orthodox Church surrounds the feast of the Baptism of Our Lord (Epiphany or Theophany) with a quite special veneration. In accordance with the ancient Christian tradition, she rates Epiphany above Christmas, which she regards as a comparatively private event. She also calls Epiphany the "Feast of the Jordan" ; on that day she blesses water and gives it to the faithful to drink. The prayers of the Orthodox

---

[1] Ignatius, *Ephes.*, XVII, 2.

"Great Blessing of the Water" (*megas hagiasmos*) express a complete theology. The Orthodox Church associates the mystery of the Water with the mysteries of Light and illumination (*photismos*). Therefore Epiphany is also called the "Feast of Lights". This last aspect is very important. It could rightly be said that Orthodox mysticism is a "Light-mysticism". The Greek notion of the "glory" (*doxa*), and the Glory, as a luminous effulgence of God, as a manifestation of His indwelling or Presence (the rabbinic *Shekinah*), is a common property of both Jewish and Christian Greek mysticism. Neither Hesychasm nor the Orthodox emphasis on Transfiguration and Resurrection can be understood if one fails to grasp the conceptions of *phōs* and *doxa*, not only as spiritual realities but as visible phenomena. In the case of Baptism, the insistence on Light and illumination averts the danger of a sacramental water-materialism and proclaims that it is the spiritual Christ who is to be appreciated.

Contact with the Lord Jesus as the Baptizer as well as the very Water of Life is the starting point of our whole spiritual life.

(2) *Baptismal grace*

St. Cyril of Jerusalem writes : "Water is at the origin of the world, the Jordan is at the origin of the Gospels."

Baptismal grace is the "first grace", i.e. the grace that communicates to man life in Christ. This grace is not only given once in Baptism. It is continued through the whole life of man ; it may be lost and recovered under the name of "sanctifying grace", the grace which keeps us united with God ; and it must be distinguished from the transitory graces granted as special helps in particular needs. The infusion or recovery (after sin) of sanctifying or baptismal grace is identical with the supernatural process called justification, regeneration, conversion or re-birth.

The Holy Spirit is given in the Baptism of Water.   Therefore the mystery of Baptism is not only a baptism with water,
but a baptism with or of the Spirit.   However, this gift of
the Spirit ought to be distinguished from the Pentecostal
grace, of which we shall speak later on.

Baptismal grace is not limited to the external ministration
of the sacrament of Baptism.   Our Lord invisibly grants
that grace to souls of good will who, consciously or even un-
consciously, are longing for the Water of Life.   This has been
called "baptism of desire".   A heathen or an atheist may
receive it.   He may long for, or indeed possess, the reality of
God without having a name for it, or even while rejecting
the name which he does not feel able to associate with the
reality.   A man who, without being baptized with water,
sacrifices his life as a witness to the Lord, receives the
"baptism of blood".

The Gospel speaks of a "baptism of fire" (Luke 3. 16, 17).
Some Fathers have understood that expression not as a
baptism with the Holy Ghost, but of the burning up of the
chaff "with unquenchable fire".   Origen, Lactantius, St.
Hilary and St. Ambrose think that these words allude to
ultimate purification of individual souls and the final
destruction of sin.

In the Orthodox rite of Baptism, as well as in baptismal
grace or baptismal life in a wide sense, we may distinguish
three fundamental elements :

(1) liberation from the yoke of Satan, or Christ forgiving
and healing ;

(2) the creation of the new man, or Christ conforming to
Himself, the pattern and archetype ;

(3) incorporation into Christ.

Now every one of these three elements includes an ascetical
and a mystical moment.   The ascetical moment is represented by a renunciation, or a promise, or a practical effort.
The mystical moment is represented by an exorcism, or an

unction, or an immersion, or a grace imparted without any external sign.

As we shall see later on, penance, unction of the sick, the first monastic profession and a second wedding are, in the mind of the Orthodox Church, extensions of baptismal grace. Moreover, at any moment, every Christian can renew or revive in himself the grace of his baptism by an orientation of his inner attitude and prayer towards that goal.

(3) *The forgiving and healing Christ*

Our Lord's first words of teaching were "The kingdom of God is at hand : repent ye . . ." (Mark 1. 15). To this repentance (*metanoia*) of man corresponds the remission of sins by the Lord Jesus, who came "to save that which was lost" (Matt. 18. 11). The forgiving Christ is one with the baptizing Christ. This inseparableness of repentance, baptism and absolution was indicated by the Apostle Peter when, to the Jews, "pricked in their hearts" and asking : "What shall we do ? " he answered : "Repent, and be baptized every one of you in the name of Jesus Christ for the remission of sins" (Acts 2. 38).

Man must be, first of all, freed from Satan's power. Jesus, during His earthly life, expelled devils. In the Orthodox rites of Baptism, this liberating action of Christ is expressed in the denial of Satan by the catechumens and in the exorcisms of the priest. The exorcism, under its diverse aspects (ritual formulæ, informal prayers, laying on of hands), may be renewed in the course of life. St. Cyril of Jerusalem writes : "Receive the exorcisms with devotion. . . . Divine exorcisms, borrowed from the Scripture, purify the soul." [1] The powers of darkness constitute an important factor in our spiritual fight. The temptations of our Lord in the desert were closely linked with His own Baptism. We should be careful not to overlook the reality

[1] *Cat.* IX, *P.G.* XXXIII, 347–350.

and the strength of objective Evil and, while dissociating it from childish caricatures, become able to discern the genuine and Biblical features of the Prince of this world. He is not devoid of an apparent beauty and nobleness. He is dangerous, not so much because of his gross appeals to the flesh as by the pride and despair which he can suggest under the forms of philosophy, art, culture, and so on. The sinister words of Descartes, *larvatus prodeo*, express exactly this masked entrance of Satan upon the scene of the world.

To the inner repentance—the "being pricked in the heart" of which the Scripture speaks—God answers by His forgiveness : "Though your sins be as scarlet, they shall be white as snow ; though they be red like crimson they shall be as wool" (Isa. i. 18). Besides this inner Penance, which is necessary in all cases, the Orthodox Church uses external Penance (*exomologesis*). The Church Canons prescribe a public Penance, or public confession of sins, for three categories of sins : idolatry, murder, adultery. Public Penance is now seldom in use. Private Penance, or secret confession to a priest, who absolves and sometimes enjoins a "medicinal penalty" (*epitimia*), is in use in most of the Orthodox Churches, although, in some of them, it has more or less fallen into desuetude. Notwithstanding a very ancient and honoured tradition, notwithstanding local regulations and an almost general practice, there is no Canon of an Œcumenical Council acknowledged as such by the Orthodox Church, which binds in duty all the faithful to use private confession, as was done in the Latin Church by the Lateran Council of 1215. On the other hand, the canons of the ancient Councils prescribing public Penance are theoretically still in force.

The Holy Mystery of Penance is a sharing in baptismal grace. It is much more : it is "a new Baptism". This is emphatically declared in the words of the Ritual, when the priest says to the penitent : "Thou hast received a new

Baptism according to the Christian mystery." The priest
who hears an *exomologesis* is not, as in the Latin Church,
a "judge". He tells the penitent : "Christ is here before
thee, invisibly present . . . I am but a witness." This is
illustrated by the corporal attitude. The Penitent, instead
of kneeling near a seated priest, stands in front of the book
of the Gospels, or the Cross, or an ikon of Christ, while
the priest stands slightly aside. The traditional Orthodox
formula of absolution is impetrative, not declarative,—
"Let God forgive thee" and not "I forgive thee" ; modern
departures from this formula, e.g. in the Russian Church,
come from Latin influence (through Poland and Ukraine).
It might be said that, in the mystery of Penance, the avowal
and the will to amend represent the ascetical element. The
absolution is the mystical element of the *exomologesis*.

In early monasticism and in the Byzantine Middle Ages
the "spiritual fathers" (*pateres pneumatikoi*) who received
confessions were not necessarily priests. They often were
lay monks. The Patriarch Nicephorus and Symeon the New
Theologian say clearly that a priest or a monk who is not a
priest can equally hear confessions,[1] and, so they seem to
imply, give absolution as well. The Orthodox Church has
reserved absolution to priests. But, even nowadays, the
practice recommended by St. James, "Confess your faults
one to another," has lost nothing of its spiritual value.

The most moving Orthodox expression of the feelings of
repentance and forgiveness may be found in the liturgical
compositions called "the Great Canon of St. Andrew of
Crete" and "the Station of St. Mary of Egypt", used during
Lent. The instruction in the Russian Ritual entitled "What
a spiritual father ought to be" should also be read.

Whatever form Penance may take, it must always be a
breaking of the heart at the feet of Christ.

[1] Symeon the N. Th. "Discourse on Exomologesis", published by
Holl in *Enthusiasmus und Bussgewalt*. See also the collection of canons
(*syntagmata*) edited by Rhalle and Polti.

The "gift of tears" or "way of tears" is connected with baptismal and penitential grace. We could find in the Orthodox East an important theology of tears. The holy sadness "steeping our very thought in tears" (Diadochus), purifies and illuminates. St. John Damascene, in his treatise *On the Orthodox Faith*, numbers tears among the forms of Baptism. St. Symeon the New Theologian calls them the Baptism of the Holy Spirit ; indeed he considers that sins committed after Baptism cannot be forgiven without tears. St. John Climacus does not hesitate to write : "The flood of tears which we shed after our Baptism, that is, after the former infant Baptism, is yet more powerful than Baptism itself—bold as this assertion may appear. For Baptism cleanses only from offences previously committed, tears from offences after Baptism . . . If God, in His mercy, had not granted to men this second baptism, then few indeed would be saved." [1]

Nicetas Stēthatos teaches that tears can even restore lost virginity.[2] The gift of tears has not yet received from historians of Christian spirituality the attention which it deserves. We have yet much to learn of the blessed way shown to men, long ago, by Mary of Magdala.

Monastic profession has been considered in the East a "second Baptism". St. Theodore the Studite and others after him classify monastic profession among the sacraments. This identification of Baptism with monastic profession even received an official consecration in Byzantine law.[3] The baptismal and penitential character of monastic initiation is expressed by the rites of the first profession. But the second profession, or reception of the "great and angelic habit", is, as we shall see, more connected with the grace of Transfiguration and the Eucharist.

The Orthodox rite of second marriage is a penitential rite.

[1] See Hieromonk Lev, "The gift of tears", in *Sobornost* (Dec. 1937).
[2] *P.G.* CXX, 933.
[3] 5th *Novella* of the Emperor Justinian.

The Orthodox Church, in principle, does not approve of a second wedding. The rules of the Patriarch Nicephorus deprived twice-married people of communion for two years and for five years the thrice married. The liturgical texts for the second wedding replace the coronation (*stephanōsis*) of the husband and wife by a kind of penitential service in which we read stern words like these : "It is better to marry in the Lord than to burn. . . . They, being unable to bear the heat and burden of the day and the hot desires of the flesh. . . . Vouchsafe unto them the contribution of the Publican, the tears of the harlot, the confession of the thief." But we must remember that, according to the beautiful image of Hermas in his *Shepherd*, the Angel of Penitence has also the features of a tender Shepherd.

The baptizing Christ heals and forgives. Jesus "went about . . . healing all manner of sickness and all manner of disease among the people" (Matt. 4. 23). "He said to His disciples : Heal the sick that are therein, and say unto them, The Kingdom of God is come nigh unto you" (Luke 10. 9).

The Orthodox Church follows the rules laid down by St. James : "Is any sick among you ? let him call for the elders of the church ; and let them pray over him, anointing him with oil in the name of the Lord : and the prayer of faith shall save the sick, and the Lord shall raise him up ; and if he have committed sins, they shall be forgiven him" (James 5. 14, 15). The mystery of Unction, in the Orthodox Church, is a joint mystery of bodily healing and of remission of sins. In order to make it clear that Christ Himself, and not any delegated minister, forgives the sick man, the priest lays the book of the Gospels open on the sick man's head and says : "It is not my sinful hand, but the very hand of God that is now stretched upon thee." The gift of healing may, of course, be exercised outside the sacrament of the Unction. The gift, with its two-fold aspect, is part and parcel of the spiritual life.

(4) *The re-creating Christ*

Baptismal grace takes away original sin, and penitential grace, the extension of Baptism, blots out actual sin. But the baptizing Christ performs yet another work. He restores the primitive order abolished by sin, and creates a new man : "Put on the new man, which after God is created in righteousness and true holiness" (Eph. 4. 24). St. Irenaeus, St. Basil, St. Gregory of Nyssa, and St Cyril of Alexandria teach that the Lord Jesus—the new Adam—gives us back the State of integrity possessed by the first Adam before his fall.

This work of re-creation is expressed, in the Holy Mystery of baptism, by the unctions performed with the "oil of catechumens" before the immersion. It is not yet Baptism, properly speaking, but a necessary preparation for it. Only the restored, re-created man can be united to Christ. The unction with the oil of catechumens means that the sinner is replaced in the state of original integrity : now he can be incorporated into Christ in the baptismal water. This unction differs, of course, from the Chrismation which, after baptism, communicated Pentecostal grace. The oil of catechumens is not the Chrism ; it has, nevertheless, its special effect. It "purifies, by burning them, the traces of sin," says St. Cyril of Jerusalem.[1] The priest, when he blesses this oil, calls it an "anointing into incorruption . . . renewing the soul and the body." He anoints the ears for "the hearing of faith" ; he anoints the hands, saying "Thy hands have made me and fashioned me"; he anoints the feet, that they may "walk in the way of the commandments." A new man, ready to be baptized, has now been created. This preliminary and re-creative aspect of Baptism is too often overlooked.

Isaias the Younger says : "When God created man, He placed him in paradise, having his senses whole and set in

[1] *Cat.* XX, 3 ; *P.G.* XXIII.

nature" (i.e. in the state wherein the reason given by God dominates the will) ; "and when man heard the one who had met him" (i.e. the Tempter) "all his senses turned against nature." [1] This conception of "nature" is very important. The state of nature is not the state of man as he comes into this world—man at his birth ; the true state of nature, *physis*, is the paradisal state. Sins are conditions alien to nature, *paraphyseis.* The normal nature of man is to be " after the nature of Adam" (*kata physin tou Adam*) or, better still, "after the nature of Jesus" (*kata physin tou Jēsou*). These are the very words of Abbot Isaias. Again, he says : "If man does not reach what is according to the nature of the Son of God, all his labours are in vain." [2] Thus, before considering our incorporation into Christ, we must consider our relationship with Him as archetype and prototype of human nature.

Orthodox ascetism cannot be understood, unless the Orthodox conception of "integral" human nature, created after the pattern of Christ's nature, is fully grasped. The word *metanoia*, "repentance", literally means "change of mind". The task is to come back from a corrupt to the pure or primitive state of mind. This process has been set by the Greek Fathers in the context of a very definite psychology. How did they conceive the structure of the human soul ? St. Paul had already distinguished between the vital principle (*psyche*) and the thinking principle (*pneuma*) and opposed the *pneumatikos*, or spiritual man, to the *psychikos*, or man of instincts governed by his feelings. St. Augustine established a similar opposition between *animus* and *mens*. Plato had distinguished between the body (*soma*), the soul (*psyche*) and the mind (*nous*). The *nous* is the rational element (*logikon, rationabile*) within us. It is synonymous with heart (*kardia*) for, according to the Greeks,

---

[1] 29 *Logoi* of Isaias the Younger, *P.G.* LX, 1105–1206.
[2] *Hom.* 19. 2.

the heart represented not the life of feelings, but a lofty life of intellect and reasonable will. The *nous*, as one of the Fathers, Evagrius, explains, begets the *phronēsis* or *rectum judicium*, the right practical judgment. The opposite to the *nous* is lack of balance in all its forms, unruly and inordinate passion. The essential malice of passion consists in the fact that it is an excess (the *nimietas*, "too much", of the Latins). The passionate man no longer controls his being ; he is acted upon (*pati, passio*). "The *nous*", says St. Athanasius, "is the mirror of the Logos. How easily can this mirror be tarnished" ! According to Origen, asceticism is to make the *nous* dominant over the whole man : the entire soul must become *nous*.

Here begins the spiritual fight, the "good fight", or, according to a strikingly Greek expression of St. Paul, the "beautiful fight" (*ton agōna ton kalon*, 2 Tim. 4. 7). Even after baptism, there will always be a tension between the tempted man and his prototype, Christ. St. John Chrysostom, picking up a metaphor of St. Paul's, considers the oil of catechumens as the unction of the athletes. Cassian, Evagrius, St. Nilus, Hesychius, have classified the main sins : *gastrimargia* or gluttony, *porneia* or impurity, *phylargyria* or covetousness, *kenodoxia* or vainglory, *lupe* or melancholy (*acedia* of the Latin tradition), *katalalia* or slander, *orge* and *oxycholia* or irascibility, *pikria* or bitterness. All can be reduced to the three fundamental lusts—lust of the flesh, lust of the eyes, pride of life—of which St. John speaks (1 John 2. 16) and which are but various aspects of one egoism : the self-assertion of the separated. Each of those sins is a passion, *thymos*, an excess that suffocates the *nous* and mutilates or even destroys within us the likeness of Jesus our archetype. How shall we be able to maintain in ourselves the new man and the soberness of the Logos ? The Eastern tradition recommends four main ascetical methods : the custody of the heart, continence, fasting and alms-giving.

The custody of the heart, chiefly insisted on by Hesychius, is a strict and permanent control of the imagination.

Continence has always been an ideal of the Orthodox Church. This point must be made quite clear. In itself, sexual activity, directed towards the multiplication of the children of God and controlled by the Logos, is entirely good. In fact, human nature being weakened by the fall (even after the forgiveness of original sin), it is extremely seldom that sexual activity is really exercised under divine guidance. In most cases the exercise of that activity implies an inner "catastrophe" (in the original meaning of the word : subversion, overturning) and a predominance of the flesh over the Logos. The union of man and woman is not such in the intention of God ; a true marriage, implying a sexual life in Christ, might be a real state of perfection and we shall see, later on, how it should be an extension of the Paschal grace.

But are such unions in the majority or are they rare exceptions? The answer to this question has led the Church to consider the way of continence as in practice a safer means to perfection. Moreover, continence, chosen for Christ's sake and in accordance with His example, acquires a sacrificial excellency. For these reasons the whole patristic and ecclesiastical tradition has proclaimed the superiority of virginity and celibacy over marriage. The Church has rejected the opinion of those who considered continence and marriage as two ways of equal value and reduced the whole question to a question of "vocations". The duty of answering the individual call does not abolish the objective scale of values of the Church. When Jovinian, of whom Harnack said that he was "a protestant before the letter", [1] taught, about the end of the fourth century, that virginity and marriage are, in themselves, equally good and meritorious, the Church condemned and excommunicated him (decision of Pope Siricius, approved by St. Ambrose and St. Jerome ; Synods of Rome

---

[1] I.e. before the technical term existed.

and Milan, *c.* 390). Such was the standpoint of the ancient Church ; such remains the standpoint of the Orthodox Church, as well as of the Roman Church, and this opposition of outlook (which raises the questions of asceticism and monasticism) divides, perhaps even more effectively than other doctrinal differences, Eastern Orthodoxy from Protestantism and from the majority of Anglicans. The Orthodox Church blesses marriage, just as our Lord sanctified the wedding at Cana, but she repeats with our Lord : "There be eunuchs, which have made themselves eunuchs for the kingdom of heaven's sake. He that can give room (*dunamenos khorein*) to this, let him do it" (Matt. 19. 12). The Orthodox Church repeats after St. Paul: "If thou marry, thou hast not sinned," but, after him again, she says : "I would have you without carefulness. He that is unmarried careth for the things that belong to the Lord. . . . He that giveth her not in marriage doeth better" (1 Cor. 7. 28, 32, 38). And she has learnt from the book of Revelation that the virgins "follow the Lamb whithersoever He goeth" (Rev. 14. 4).

Another opinion of Jovinian condemned by the Church was that the use of food with thanksgiving is as good as fasting. The Orthodox Church is somewhat strict in the matter of fasting. She remembers the words of Jesus (which we take to be authentic): "This kind (of devil) goeth not out but by prayer and fasting" (Matt. 17. 21) and "The days will come, when the bridegroom shall be taken from them (the children of the bridechamber), and then shall they fast" (Matt. 9. 15). But the Church also remembers Isaiah's warning : "Is not this the fast that I have chosen ? to loose the bands of wickedness, to undo the heavy burdens, and to let the oppressed go free, and that ye break every yoke ? Is it not to deal thy bread to the hungry . . .? " (Isa. 58. 6, 7). Therefore the Church does not separate the precept of fasting from the precept of alms-giving. Hermas, in his *Shepherd*, had already formulated this principle : "Thou shalt set aside the amount of food which thou art used to eat every day and thou shalt give it to the widow, the orphan and the poor ; in this manner thou shalt accomplish the mortification of thy soul." St. John Chrysostom insists on the great precept of almsgiving. Addressing himself to those who adorn the table of Christ with golden vessels, when Christ Himself, in the persons of His poor, is dying from starvation, he says : "We ought to attend to one and to the other but to the other [the poor] first. This temple [the poor] is greater than the other temple." [1] To those who say : "I would whole-heartedly receive Paul in my house," he answers : "Behold the Lord of Paul can lodge in thy house, if thou wilt." [2] And again : "This altar [the poor] thou canst see raised everywhere in the streets, and thou canst at every hour, sacrifice on it . . ." [3] St. Tikhon spoke in similar words.

Origen enumerates the following stages in the fight for the supremacy of the Logos. In beginners, the revolts of the flesh begin to lose something of their violence. In proficients, they are wearing themselves out. In the perfect, they are extinct.

The whole asceticism of the Orthodox Church may be said to be expressed in the prayer of St. Ephrem which is recited in all the Lenten services : "O Lord and Master of my life, grant me not a spirit of slothfulness, of discouragement, of lust of power, of vain babbling.

"But vouchsafe unto Thy servant the spirit of continence, of meekness, of patience and of love.

"Yea, Lord and King, grant that I may perceive my own transgressions and judge not my brother."

Are the purifications which St. John of the Cross calls "the night of the senses" and "night of the spirit" mentioned in the tradition of the Orthodox Church ? Yes, though in a less precise and less technical manner. St. John of the

---

[1] *In Matt.* hom. L. [2] *In Act.* hom. XLV. [3] *In II Cor.* hom. XX.

Cross himself observes that the pseudo-Dionysius calls contemplation a "ray of darkness". For the light received in contemplation exceeds the strength of the imperfectly illuminated soul and obscures her natural perceptions. An excess of light dazzles and blinds just as an excess of darkness does. Those "nights" are connected with baptismal grace and constitute the introduction to Pentecostal illumination. It is true that Eastern spirituality has not much emphasized the night of the soul. But we must here remember some profound remarks made by Maritain. He writes that the passive purifications described by St. John of the Cross are the normal and typical forms of contemplation, its purest paradigms, which can be experienced only in contemplative cloisters. But these nights of the soul "can be made up for by other trials, caused by events or by men, and which play a similar purifying part." [1] These are the "atypical" forms of contemplation, familiar to most souls. "These souls, whose style of life is active, will have the grace of contemplation, but of a masked, unapparent contemplation. . . . The mysterious contemplation will not be in their prayer, but perhaps in the gentleness of their hands, or in their way of walking, or in the eye with which they look at a poor or suffering man." [2]

All these considerations on sins, virtues, and the inner fight represent a somewhat inferior aspect of spiritual life, if they are not distinctly connected with the Person of our Lord. As St. Paul so often and so powerfully repeated, a living Person has been substituted for the law. The law simultaneously subsists and is abolished in Christ—as a river at the same time subsists and is abolished in the sea where it loses itself. The secret of every spiritual victory is to look at the Lord Jesus, not at temptations and obstacles. As long as the Apostle Peter looked to his Master, he was

[1] *Questions de conscience*, Paris, essay : "Action et contemplation", p. 152.
[2] *Ibidem*, pp. 145–146.

able to walk on the sea ; but, when his attention turned to the struggling waves, he began to sink. A loving and constant look at the Person of Jesus is the shortest and surest ascetical method.

Is the idea of the imitation of Christ alien to the Orthodox Church ? It is often said that the notion of *imitatio Christi* is a product of the Western Middle Ages and does not belong to the Orthodox mind. This assertion is superficial and untrue. St. Basil laid strong emphasis upon the *mimesis Christou*, i.e. the imitation of Christ by the Christian, and not only in a general sense ("Have this mind in you which was also in Christ Jesus"; Phil. 2. 5, 20; 1 Cor. 4. 16, 11. 1), but in the sense of a reproduction of the deeds and words of the Saviour by ourselves. St. Basil writes : "This imitation confers on us an admirable manner of life." And again : "every action and every word of our Lord is a rule." [1] St. Gregory Nazianzen develops the same idea. We must, according to him, discover the actual and present aspect of each of Christ's gestures : the episodes of His life —e.g. the episodes connected with the Magi, the money-changers in the Temple, the Canaanite woman, Lazarus— must become episodes of our own life ; Jesus slept in order to bless our sleep, He was tired in order to bless our toils, He wept in order to bless our tears.

Vladimir Soloviev expressed a similar conception very forcibly : "Before every important decision, let us evoke in our soul the image of Christ. Let us concentrate our attention upon it and ask ourselves : Would He Himself do this action ? Or, in other words : Will He approve of it or not ? To all I propose this rule ; it does not deceive. In every dubious case, as soon as the possibility of a choice is offered to you, remember Christ. Picture to yourselves His living Person, as it really is, and entrust Him with the burden of your doubts. Let men of good will, as

[1] *Lib. de Spiritu sancto*, XIX.

individuals, as social factors, as leaders of men and peoples, apply this criterion, and they will really be able, in the name of truth, to show others the way towards God." [1]

(5) *Our incorporation into Christ*

Our conformation to Jesus, as the pattern of restored human nature does not exhaust the fullness of baptismal grace. We are saved not only by Christ, and with Christ, but in Christ. Christian life is more than Christocentrism : it is Christification. This "in Christ" aspect (the *en Christō*, which comes over and over again in St. Paul's Epistles) is sacramentally represented by baptismal immersion. The Orthodox Church, like the ancient Church and the present Baptist Churches, plunges the new Christian into the water. The immersion means death with Christ ; the emergence means risen life in Him : "Know ye not, that so many of us as were baptized into Jesus Christ were baptized into His death ? Therefore we are buried with Him by baptism into death ; that like as Christ was raised up from the dead by the glory of the Father, even so we also should walk in newness of life" (Rom. 6. 3, 4). And : "As many of you as have been baptized into Christ have put on Christ" (Gal. 3. 27).

Our membership in the Body of Christ must be understood realistically. In the phrase, the "mystical" Body of Christ, "mystical" does not mean symbolic or metaphysical and is not opposed to "physical". It means secret and invisible (cf. *mysterion*). We invisibly share in our Lord's nature (*physis*, therefore it is a "physical" Body, though not material, as ours are). This real membership of Christ was as much emphasized by the Eastern Fathers as it was in the West by St. Augustine. "What has not been assumed has not been healed" says St. Gregory Nazianzen.[2] "The Logos was already Christ and Lord.

---

[1] Soloviev, *Conclusion of the Spiritual Foundations of life.*
[2] Letter to Cledonius.

He that is assumed becomes it," writes St. Gregory of Nyssa.[1] Consider the boldness of these words : we become Christ and Lord. Chrysostom insists : the baptized Christian is not only born of God, but has put on Christ ; and this not only morally, through charity, but in reality. The Incarnation (*ensarkōsis*) has rendered our incorporation into Christ and our divinization (*theōsis*) possible. St. Methodius of Olympus writes : "Every one of us must confess not only that His coming into the flesh, which He has taken from the pure Virgin, is holy, but also a similar coming into the mind of each of us."[2] Long before this St. Irenaeus, developing the Epistle to the Ephesians, had already formulated his grand conception of the "recapitulation" of all men in Christ (*anakephalaiosis*). The Byzantine mystics do not speak otherwise than the early Greek Fathers. St. Symeon the New Theologian, in his *Divine Hymns of Love*, writes : "We become Christ's limbs or members, and Christ becomes our members. . . . Unworthy though I be, my hand and foot are Christ. I move my hand, and my hand is wholly Christ, for God's divinity is united inseparably to me. I move my foot, and lo ! it glows like God Himself . . ."

The same St. Symeon, speaking of his own particular father, Symeon the Venerable or the Studite, says that this holy monk "was not ashamed of the limbs or members of any man, neither was he afraid of seeing men naked, nor to be seen without clothes himself. For he possessed Christ wholly and was himself wholly Christ ; and he always contemplated his own limbs or members and those of any other human beings as Christ's."[3] The Pauline doctrine "Now ye are the Body of Christ, and members in particular" (1 Cor. 12. 27) must not, of course, be understood as identity of essence between the Uncreated and the created, but as an "accidental" union, granted by grace. This doctrine

---

[1] *Antirrh. adv. Apollin.*, 53.   [2] *De sanguisuga*, VIII.
[3] Quoted by S. Bulgakov in *Sobornost*, June 1935, p. 7.

throws a new light on certain modes of speech of Paul. The Apostle does not say "Christ gives life," but "To me *to live is* Christ (Phil. 1. 21) . . . life eternal in Christ Jesus (Rom. 6. 23) . . . When *Christ, our life,* shall appear (Col. 3. 4)." He does not say : "Christ gives us wisdom and righteousness, Christ sanctifies and redeems us," but : "Christ Jesus, who of God *is made* unto us *wisdom,* and *righteousness,* and *sanctification,* and *redemption*" (1 Cor. 2. 30). There is here more than the Hebraic predilection for substantives. We can speak of Christ in substantives, discarding adjectives and verbs, because He is the substance of our spiritual life.

The deep awareness of our identity with Christ which Eastern Christians had acquired explains some of the resistance to the definition of Chalcedon. If the distinction between the divine and the human natures of Christ is always to be maintained, thought these simple Christians, will our incorporation to Christ not remain incomplete ? Will our ascetical life not lose its aim ? They innocently failed to see that Godhead and mankind meet, not in a confusion of the two natures, but in the life of the one indivisible Person of our Lord.

The Orthodox Church frequently reminds her faithful of the doctrine of the Mystical Body. During the Eucharistic Liturgy of the chief feasts, at the time of the "Little Entrance", the people sing, instead of the Trisagion, the words of St. Paul : "As many of you as have been baptized into Christ have put on Christ."

(6) *The spring of the soul*

This relationship established between our Lord and the human soul is most intimate. It must not, however, be mistaken for the full summer of spiritual life. It is the transition from the winter of sin to the spring of the redeemed existence. It is the morning dawn, not the splendour of noon. The green buds blow, the flowers open, but the

fruits are not yet ripe. It is a spiritual adolescence, sometimes anxious and emotional, full of transports and outbursts,
yet not without timidity and hesitation—and seldom without
falls—but always with a keen feeling of discovery and the
breathing in of a great breeze of hope. Piety then assumes
a strongly affective colouring. The words of the Song of
Songs (those expressing the quest rather than the full union)
become actual : "Draw me, we will run after thee (i. 4) ; As
a lily among thorns, so is my love among the daughters . . .
He brought me to the banqueting house, and his banner
over me was love . . . The voice of my Beloved ! behold, he
cometh . . . For, lo, the winter is past, the rain is over and
gone ; the flowers appear on the earth (2. 2, 4, 8, 11, 12)."

These times of Baptism, of Penance, of conversion, of
healing and forgiveness, are the blessed times of the first
meeting, or of a new meeting, with the Lord Jesus. Thus
after His own Baptism our Lord met His first disciples :
"What seek ye ? . . . Master, where dwellest thou ? . . .
Come and see . . . They came and saw where he dwelt, and
abode with him that day . . ." (John. 1. 38, 39). But, as
St. Basil reminds us, "it is not thou that hadst seized Christ
by thy virtue, but Christ seized thee by His coming."[1] The
early Church expressed this baptismal newness and freshness
of life in graceful symbols ; the white robe of the neophytes,
the milk and honey offered to them, the lighted candle placed
in their hands. To this spring of the soul belongs the image
of the tender and handsome Shepherd (*ho poimēn ho kalos*)
who brings back the lost sheep on his shoulders. But the
regeneration through water, or rather the gift which water
signifies, is usually expressed by the divine Fish or *Ichthys*,[2]
which we find on so many early Christian monuments :

"Celestial race of the divine Ichthys, strengthen thy

---

[1] *Hom.* 20.
[2] The Greek word *Ichthys* means "fish". Besides the symbolical
complex "Christ-water-fish", *Ichthys* is the acrostic of *Jesous
Christos Theou Huios Sōtēr* (Jesus Christ, son of God, Saviour).

heart, since thou hast received, amidst the mortals, the immortal source of the divine water. Gladden, therefore, thy soul by the ever-springing water of the Wisdom that gives the treasuries. Take this food, sweet as the honey of the Saviour of the saints ; eat with delight, holding in thy hands the Ichthys."[1]

[1] From the famous Christian Greek inscription called "The Inscription of Pectorius" at Autun (France).

CHAPTER IV

CHRIST THE SENDER OF THE SPIRIT

(1) *The grace of Pentecost*

IN EARLY CHRISTIAN art, we often find the dove standing by
a vase full of water and holding in her beak an olive branch.
The grace of Pentecost follows on and completes the grace
of Baptism. Therefore the Eastern Church, abiding by the
primitive tradition, confers the gift of the Holy Ghost
immediately after Baptism.

Between Water and Spirit there exists a link which the
whole of Scripture suggests. After the Creation, "the
Spirit of God moved on the face of the waters" (Gen. 1. 2).
After the Flood, the dove came to Noah, having "in her
mouth an olive leaf" (Gen. 8. 11), the symbol of unction.
After the Baptism of Jesus, "the heavens were open unto
him, and he saw the Spirit of God descending like a dove"
(Matt. 3. 16). But the coming of the "cloven tongues like
as of fire" on the disciples at Pentecost (Acts 2. 3) was the
most striking expression of the descent of the Holy Ghost
on Christians. Once more we meet here the luminous or
fiery manifestation of God, "glory", *doxa*, so important in
Helleno-Christian mysticism.

The Orthodox Church has made "Chrisma" (i.e. the
equivalent of the Latin Confirmation) the external expression
of the mystery of our participation in the Holy Spirit. But,
just as baptismal grace extends beyond the sacrament of
Baptism in the strict sense, the gift of the Holy Ghost
cannot be exclusively identified with Chrisma. Scripture
points to cases when the Spirit was given without any human
ministration : such was the case of Cornelius and others
(Acts 10. 44). There were cases when the Spirit was poured

out before Baptism, either directly (in the case of Cornelius) or through a laying-on of hands (in the case of Saul (Acts 9. 17). It happened also that the Spirit came a second time on a group which had already received it (Acts 5. 31). In many modern cases we should not dare to deny the reality of a "Baptism of the Spirit" conferred upon men who had not received it sacramentally. "The wind bloweth where it listeth" (John 3. 8), and "God giveth not the Spirit by measure" (John 3. 34).

The grace of the Spirit, of course, is already active in the baptism with water, as well as the grace of the Father and the grace of the Son. But there is a special sending of the Spirit to man ; and a Baptism with water not completed by the Baptism with the Holy Ghost would manifest a deficient Christian life. "Ye shall be baptized with the Holy Ghost," said our Lord (Acts 11. 16). The question of Paul to the Ephesian disciples, "Did ye receive the Holy Ghost ?" (Acts 19. 2) is asked of every one of us. It would not be enough to answer : I have received the mystery or sacrament of the Spirit after my Baptism, when I was anointed with the holy Chrism. The question is whether and how this seed of the Spirit has been afterwards developed within the soul.

It is sometimes difficult to discern the proper part of the Holy Ghost in the Christian life. The action of the Holy Spirit cannot be separated from the action of the Son. There is no place, in the Orthodox Church, for belief in a "third kingdom" or Kingdom of the Spirit succeeding to the Kingdom of Christ. Those who speak of an Orthodox "pnèumatocentrism" opposed to the so-called "Christo-centrism" of the Roman Church may express their personal theology, but they speak a language alien to the Fathers and to the Orthodox saints. When we ascribe a definite action to the Spirit or to the Son, or to the Father, we are using, as the Latins say, "appropriations" (to these "appropriations" correspond the Greek *klēseis*). But the Father and the Son

are included in every action of the Spirit. The three Persons share in the activity of each of them. Leaving aside
the question of the *Filioque* (which was to a great extent a
misunderstanding and does not present insuperable
obstacles), we must notice two important points. On the
one hand, it is the Lord Jesus who sends the Spirit to men :
"When the Comforter is come, whom I will send unto you
from the Father (John 15. 26) . . . If I depart, I will
send him [the Comforter] unto you (John 16. 7) . . . He
breathed on them and saith unto them : Receive ye the Holy
Ghost (John 20. 22)." On the other hand, our Lord is not
the origin only, but the goal of the mission of the Spirit :
"The Spirit of truth . . . shall not speak of himself, but
whatsoever he shall hear, that shall he speak. . . . He
shall glorify me : for he shall receive of mine, and shall
shew it unto you" (John 16. 13, 14). After Pentecost as
before, the Lord Jesus—as the Son, therefore as directing
Himself and us, but us in Him, towards the Father—
remains the "object" of spiritual life. The Spirit is the
means and, being immanent in our soul, the "subject" of
that life. The "subject" strives towards the "object".
The Spirit forms Christ within us and renders Him present
to us. If we commit the mistake of looking at the Spirit
otherwise than as the Spirit who reveals Christ to us, we
cannot reach Him ; He retires and in some way vanishes.
The Holy Ghost does not replace Christ and does not serve
as His substitute, but He prepares us for Christ and achieves
in us the Parousia, the eternal coming and Presence of Jesus
the Lord.

(2) *The Anointing*

Jesus is the Messiah, i.e. the Anointed. The word
Christos, in Greek, immediately evokes the idea of *chrisma* or
unction. Our Chrismation is an extension of, and a sharing in,
the unction of Our Lord with the Holy Ghost, accomplished

by the Father.   Therefore the unction unites us not only to the Spirit, but to the Son.   The Father anoints us with the Holy Ghost as sons, as members of His Son.

The sacramental link between the Spirit and the oil or balsam of Chrisma or Confirmation was sometimes conceived by the Fathers as being parallel to the link between Christ and the Eucharistic elements.   St. Cyprian refers to the consecration of the Chrism as to an *eucharistia*;[1] he was perhaps only referring to the "eucharistic" form of the prayer of consecration.   St. Cyril of Jerusalem uses language suggestive of a real presence of the Holy Ghost in the Chrism. He writes: "See that you do not mistake the Chrism for mere unguent.   For, just as the bread of the Eucharist after the invocation of the Holy Spirit is not ordinary bread, so also this holy ointment is no more simple ointment after the invocation, but the gracious *charisma* of Christ and the Holy Ghost, being made operative by the presence of His Divinity."[2]   We shall notice that Cyril speaks here not only of a charism of the Holy Ghost, but of a charism of Christ and the Holy Ghost.   The chrisma is an approach to Christ through the Spirit, and thus it reveals to us the exact office of the Spirit in our life.   There is, however, a special and direct association of the Holy Ghost with the Chrism. The Orthodox Church offers no theory about the manner in which the Chrism is instrumental in making the Holy Spirit sacramentally present and operative.   But the view of St. Cyril concerning the parallelism between Chrism and Eucharist agrees with the general sacramental outlook of the Orthodox Church and deserves more of our prayerful and enquiring attention than it has yet received.   We do not think that we sin against "worship in spirit and truth." when we adore the presence and sacrifice of our Lord in the bread broken and the wine shed.   With the

----

[1] *Ep.* 70, 2.   [2] *Cat.* XXI, 3.

same realism we can adore the presence and effusion of the Holy Ghost in the anointing Chrism.

And yet we must again and again remember that "God is a Spirit: and they that worship him must worship him in spirit and in truth" (John 4. 14)—especially when we turn to the Person of the Holy Ghost. Pentecostal grace cannot, any more than Baptismal and Eucharistic grace, be fixed and, as it were, crystallized around the outward ministration of the Holy Mysteries. The Chrisma, the ritual anointing, is but the efficacious sign or *sacramentum* of the invisible and spiritual unction which God pours out in the hearts of men whenever and wherever He pleases. Two passages from the New Testament explain the nature of this unction and its relation to the Spirit and to Christ. St. Paul writes: "He that stablisheth us with you in Christ and anointed us is God, who also sealed us and gave us the earnest of the Spirit in our hearts" (2 Cor. 1. 21, 22). St. John says : "The anointing which ye received of Him abideth in you, and ye need not that any one teach you ; but as his anointing teacheth you concerning all things, and is true, and is no lie, and even as it taught you, ye abide in him" (1 John 2. 27).

(3) *The seal*

As we have just seen, St. Paul speaks of the unction as a "seal". The Book of Revelation enumerates the servants of God "sealed" from all the tribes. St. Cyril of Jerusalem writes : "Do not forget the Holy Ghost at the time of your illumination ; He is ready to stamp your soul with His seal."[1] The Eastern Church calls the mystery of the gift of the Holy Spirit not only the unction, *chrisma*, but the seal, *sphragis* (in Slavonic, *petchat*).

The word *sphragis* was much used in Christian antiquity. The *sphragis*, in technical language, was the mark

[1] *Cat.* XVII, 35; *P.G.* XXXIII, 1009.

made on the forehead either of the animals destined for the sacrifices, or of slaves, or of soldiers.   The Greek word *character* and the Latin word *signaculum* were used in same sense.   It is likely that St. Paul thought of the *sphragis* when he wrote : "I bear branded on my body the marks of the Lord Jesus" (Gal. 6. 17).   He called himself "slave [*doulos*] of Jesus Christ."

The seal is stamped on us by the Holy Ghost.   But this seal itself has reference rather to Christ.   Philo had already spoken of the Logos as being God's seal upon the world. The early Christians were familiar with the conception of Christ as the plastic image of the Father.   The sealing by the Holy Ghost means therefore that the Spirit imprints on us the Father's likeness, that is, the Lord Jesus Himself. From that moment we do not belong any more to ourselves ; we have become—according to the historical meaning of the word *Sphragis*—the slaves and the soldiers of Christ, and His sacrificial co-victims.   The first Christians used the expression "to keep the seal" (*ton sphragida terein*) in the sense of remaining faithful.

In the Orthodox Church, the priest anoints the Christian's organs of sense, saying at each anointing : "The seal of the gift of the Holy Ghost."   This action has a twofold aspect : an ascetical one and a mystical one.   The ascetical aspect, which involves our personal effort, consists in exclusive dedication and the shutting of our senses.   The seal consecrates them to Jesus Christ and closes them to everything opposed or alien to Him.   It is the same thing as the "circumcision of the heart", or the death unto ourselves, which immersion represents in Baptism.

The *sphragis* and the sealing can become a conscious phenomenon of our spiritual life long after Baptism.   We shall see later on how the sealing can be manifested in the life of prayer.   Conscious sealing (which differs from the passive sealing imparted in the Chrismation of infants) is a product of will and love : "Set me as a seal upon thine arm : for love is strong as death" (Song of Songs 8. 6). "A garden inclosed is my sister, my spouse ; a spring shut up, a fountain sealed" (*ibid*. 4. 12).

(4) *The new spiritual senses*

The negative and ascetical aspect of the *sphragis* is the closing of our senses to the things of the world, for Christ's sake. Its positive and mystical aspect, dependent no more on our effort but on grace, is the opening of our senses to realities until then unperceived, untasted. Our natural senses are transformed into new and spiritual ones : "Behold, I make all things new" (Rev. 21. 5).

This is a different process from the re-creation or restoration of fallen human nature, represented by the anointing of the catechumens before Baptism. We are amended and made fit for Baptism by the anointing with the oil of catechumens. We are united with the dying and rising Christ by the immersion into and the emergence from the water. We are, by the sealing of Chrismation, admitted to a bodily (as well as spiritual) new life, to an entirely supernatural use of our natural senses.

Once more let us remember, when we speak thus, that the oil, the water and the Chrism are but sacramental signs. The inner realities which they express, the invisible Baptism and Unction, are the "things", the *res*, beyond and above all *signa*.

St. Thomas Aquinas and the Latin mystics have described the transformation or transposition of our bodily senses which happens in mystical life. Origen had already spoken of the "spiritual senses." [1] Nicetas Stēthatos [2] has shown how the unction or sealing confers a particular mystical function on each of the five senses. To sight corresponds the gift of vision, either "intellectual" or "sensory". To

---

[1] *Hom. III super Levit.*
[2] In the 1st of his *Centuries* (chapters).

hearing corresponds the perception of "divine locutions", either purely interior words, or words received by the ear. To the lips and tongue are given the words of prophecy.   To tactile sense correspond the divine "touches" which not only the soul but the flesh experiences.   Even taste and smell become open to new perceptions.   Cassian writes : "It frequently happens, in the divine visits, that we are filled with perfumes, of a sweetness unknown to human skill ; so that the soul, overwhelmed with delight, is lifted into a rapture and forgets that she is living in the flesh." [1]   The rare scents which enter into the composition of the Orthodox Chrism symbolize these supernatural fragrances.   Scripture speaks of the sweet smell of sacrifices and of the ointment offered to Jesus, the odour of which filled the house.   St. Paul says : "We are a sweet savour of Christ unto God" (2. Cor. 2. 15).   And the Song of Songs: "Because of the savour of thy good ointments thy name is as ointment poured forth (1. 3) . . . A bundle of myrrh is my well beloved unto me (1. 13) . . . The smell of thy garments is like the smell of Lebanon" (4. 11).

To most Christians such words are mere symbols.   The average Christian (alas !) experiences difficulties in understanding the transposition of the senses on to the supernatural plane.   But the lives of saints afford ample illustration of this fact.   Even Christians who are not saints may know them episodically.   Pentecostal grace takes us far beyond the state of integrity given back to nature by the pre-baptismal unction.   Chrismation (either visibly or invisibly conferred) introduces us into charismatic life.

(5) Charismatic life

The gifts of the *Pneuma*, which marked the beginnings of the Church, are not things of the past.   They have been given, they *are* given, to the Church for all times.

[1] *Collat.* IV.

What are these "pneumatic" gifts ? Some biblical texts describe the graces of the Spirit : "And it shall come to pass afterward, that I will pour out my spirit upon all flesh ; and your sons and your daughters shall prophesy, your old men shall dream dreams, your young men shall see visions : and also upon the servants and upon the handmaids in those days will I pour out my spirit" (Joel 2. 28, 29).

"And the spirit of the Lord shall rest upon him, the spirit of wisdom and understanding, the spirit of counsel and might, the spirit of knowledge and of fear of the Lord" (Isa. 11. 2).

"The manifestation of the Spirit is given to every man to profit withal. For to one is given by the Spirit the word of wisdom ; to another the word of knowledge by the same Spirit ; to another faith by the same Spirit ; to another the gift of healing by the same Spirit; to another the working of miracles ; to another prophecy ; to another discerning of spirits ; to another divers kinds of tongues ; to another the interpretation of tongues : but all these worketh that one and the self-same Spirit, dividing to every man severally as he will" (1 Cor. 12. 7–10). "The fruit of the spirit is love, joy, peace, long-suffering, gentleness, goodness, faith, meekness, temperance : against such there is no law" (Gal. 5. 22, 23).

These enumerations or classifications should not be too rigidly adhered to. Greek theology initiated the doctrine of the seven gifts of the Holy Ghost : Clement of Alexandria, following Philo, compared the seven gifts to the seven-branched candlestick. But, on the whole, the Eastern Church has been less precise than the Latin Church (and, in particular, St. Thomas Aquinas) on these matters. She does not make a clear-cut distinction between the gifts and the fruits of the Holy Spirit. She does not draw a sharp line between the gift that sanctifies its bearer (*gratia gratum faciens* of the Latin theologians) and the charisma that edifies its witnesses without necessarily sanctifying its bearer (*gratia gratis data*). She rather inclines to believe that the charisma generally, though accessorily, leads to the sanctification of the man who holds it and that the gift generally, though accessorily, leads to the edification of other people. The Greek Fathers use as almost synonymous the words "gifts" (*doreai*), "powers" (*dynameis*), "energies" (*energeiai*), "charisms" (*charismata*). Greek Christian thought always seems reluctant to introduce rational analysis in the realm of pure grace.

The saints are the heirs and successors of the "charismatics" of the first centuries. Though holiness and hierarchical responsibility have often been associated, it is to the saint as a saint rather than to the hierarch as a hierarch that vision and prophecy seem to have been granted. These saints and prophets fulfil within the Church a pneumatic and necessary ministry. On the other hand, the Orthodox mind is unwilling to consider the local and institutional ministry, i.e. the intendants (*episkopoi*), elders (*presbyteroi*) and servants (*diakonoi*), as invested with a merely administrative and ritual office. The Spirit is given to the deacons, priests and bishops with the laying on of hands (*cheirothesis* or *cheirotonia*). Therefore all Ordinations imply some participation in Pentecostal grace, and are in some way related to Chrismation, though they have still more connection, as we shall see, with Paschal grace and the Eucharist. The full "Apostolic succession" is a transmission of the fire of Pentecost and of the life of grace of the Holy Apostles. When hierarchical office and pneumatic gifts coincide, we may have such men as, in the Greek Church, Chrysostom, Basil, the two Gregories. When there is a discrepancy between the office and the life of grace, the gifts may be reduced to merely external charisms, and we may get ecclesiastical equivalents of Caiaphas, who prophesied as "being high priest that year" (John 11. 51).

Such figures as St. Seraphim of Sarov and Father John of

Kronstadt witness to the ever-continuing action of the Holy
Ghost in the recent history of the Orthodox Church.

Only their lack of faith inclines contemporary Christians
to consider charismatic manifestations in our days exceptional.
If they are exceptional, it is because of a lack of faith similar to
that which hindered Jesus at Nazareth: "He did not do many
mighty works there because of their unbelief" (Matt. 13. 58).
But the power of the Spirit is as alive to-day as it was in the
days of the Book of Acts. The mighty works accomplished
then in the name of the Lord Jesus, *en onomati Kyriou*, and
in the strength of the Holy Ghost, can be accomplished now,
if only we had faith! "And these signs shall follow them
that believe ; in my name shall they cast out devils ; they
shall speak with new tongues . . . they shall lay hands on
the sick, and they shall recover" (Mark 16. 17, 18). "Verily,
I say unto you : he that believeth on me, the works that I
do shall he do also ; and greater works than these shall he
do" (John 14. 12).

Although "ordinary" physical causes and sequences of
phenomena may be the instrument of the Spirit, we should
not feel reluctant to acknowledge direct divine interventions,
which break the so-called natural laws. For the network of
physical laws and the determinism that it seems to involve
(occasioning as it does, catastrophes, diseases, etc.) manifests
a distortion of primitive order and results from original sin ;
this is the bondage of corruption under which "the whole
creation groaneth and travaileth in pain together until now"
(Rom. 8. 22). Saints and charismatics are the liberators of
the world. "Miracles" are a return to the primitive "free"
state of creation, i.e. a world entirely transparent to the glory
of God ; they express the normal condition of creation
before the fall, and still more after Pentecost.

The practical attitude of the Eastern Church towards
charisms is not quite identical with that of the Western
Church. The Christian West is cautious, and somewhat

reserved on the subject of extraordinary graces. It may hold them in veneration, but refrains from asking for them. The Orthodox Church, it is true, is very much upon its guard against what it calls "illusion" and "seduction". Nevertheless the Eastern mystics, chiefly the Hesychasts, do not hesitate to expect and to demand extraordinary graces. The Orthodox Church is inclined to consider charisms as the normal goal of the pneumatic life opened by Chrismation (this is made clear in the famous conversation of St. Seraphim of Sarov with Motovilov). It is in a frame of mind more realistic, perhaps, than that of the Latin Church that she listens to St. Paul's advice : "Covet earnestly the best charisms (*ta charismata ta meizona*)" (1 Cor. 12. 31), and that she repeats the prayer of the disciples : "Grant unto thy servants, that with all boldness they may speak thy word, by stretching forth thy hand to heal ; and that signs and wonders may be done by the name of thy holy child Jesus" (Acts 4. 29, 30). But the Eastern Church entirely agrees with the Western Church in refusing to consider the pneumatic gifts as an aim. They are, as St. John Chrysostom said, "helps" (*antilēmpseis*). Beyond the charisms, there is the "still more excellent way" (1 Cor. 12. 31), which the Apostle Paul announces before declaiming his hymn to charity. Beyond all the gifts there is the Spirit—whose proper name is *the* Gift.

(6) *Pentecost and Illumination*

If Baptismal grace mainly corresponds to what has been called the way or life of purification, pentecostal grace corresponds, rather, to the illuminative life. At this stage, spiritual life becomes less subjective. Our doubts, difficulties and emotional flights cease to be foremost. The anxious loving quest—"Saw ye him whom my soul loveth?" (Song of Songs 3. 3)—gives place to a feeling of quiet possession : "I held him, and would not let him go" (*ibid.*

3. 4). We open ourselves to the objective Word of God and to a process of illumination by the Light within. We become more like Mary, who "sat at Jesus' feet and heard His Word" (Luke 10. 39). Baptismal grace has already incorporated us into Christ by water. Pentecostal grace incorporates us into Him by light and fire.

We have several times mentioned the "supernatural luminous ray of divine darkness" of which the pseudo-Dionysius speaks [1] and we suggested its analogy with the night of the soul described by St. John of the Cross. Coming back to this theme, we could say that this divine darkness (Eastern terminology) or this night of the mind (Western terminology) is the threshold of Pentecostal life. We think, moreover, that the silence and suspension of faculties—the "ligature"—which, according to St. John of the Cross, mark the entrance into mystical life, could be compared with the negative aspect of the sealing or *sphragis* in which we acknowledged the first manifestation of Pentecostal life.

Although the Eastern Fathers have not distinguished with precision, as the Western theologians have, between infused virtues and gifts, we think that the outlines of such a distinction could be found in their writings. In infused, as in acquired, virtues, human effort is blended with divine co-operation, but with an overpowering prevalence of the divine element (the balance is more preserved in acquired virtues). Now in the case of gifts the instrumental causality and the mode of operation are entirely divine. The Holy Ghost intervenes directly in the soul. It is the substitution of this régime of gifts for the régime of virtues, either acquired or infused (these last marking the transition), that constitutes the mystical state. The soul then becomes, more or less continuously, as St. Gregory Nazianzen says, "an organ which the Holy Spirit blows and on which He plays."

[1] *De mystic. theol.*, I, 1, *P.G.* III.

Under the touch of the Spirit, the soul acquires an acute penetration, an inner and experimental knowledge, of divine things. This is the *sapientia* or wisdom (from *sapere*, to taste) of the Latin theologians. This wisdom is opposed to the *stultitia* or animal stupidity chiefly caused by impurity. The soul becomes a "theologian-soul" (not a "theological soul"). This deep expression "theologian-soul," *theologos psyche*, was coined by Diadochus of Photike for whom *theologia* meant divine illumination—not human discourse about God, but the word of God (*theou logos*) within us.

The discernment of spirits (*kryptognosis*), or knowledge of the hidden things (*kardiognosis* or knowledge of the heart), is next granted. St. Anthony and Cassian give to this discernment or "discretion" pre-eminence over all the virtues ; they make contact at this point with St. Benedict and St. Ignatius of Loyola.

During this season of Pentecostal grace, the Holy Spirit opens our minds to the understanding of the Scriptures. Difficulties cease to be difficulties. It matters little if Babylonian myths be found in the Book of Genesis, or nuptial poems in the Song of Songs! what matters is what the Holy Ghost has taught the Church to read into the sacred text and the interpretation which He gives of it in our hearts. A new, a quite personal and vital, relationship is formed between the Scripture and ourselves. Under the letter which rightly engrosses the historians and philologists, the Spirit reveals to us a hidden text—like the water-mark in paper—telling us of the beloved Son. Jesus had done so with the two disciples on the road to Emmaus : "He expounded unto them in all the scriptures the things concerning himself" (Luke 24. 27). The same experience may be our lot ; to us also it may be given to say : "Did not our heart burn within us, while he talked with us by the way and while he opened to us the Scriptures?" (Luke 24. 32).

The soul enlightened by Pentecostal grace lives under a

more or less habitual guidance. She is helped in her practical and daily decisions. She converses with her Lord. "He talked with us by the way . . ." She says with Samuel, "Speak, Lord ; for Thy servant heareth" (1 Sam. 3. 9). To the illuminated soul the words of the prophets come true : "After those days, saith the Lord, I will put my law in their inward parts, and write it in their hearts . . . and they shall teach no more every man his neighbour and every man his brother, saying, Know the Lord, for they shall all know me" (Jer. 31. 33, 34). "A new heart also will I give you, and a new spirit will I put within you : and I will take away the stony heart out of your flesh . . . And I will put my spirit within you" (Ezek. 36. 26, 27).

How shall we avoid the danger of mistaking our own sub-conscious for the voice of the Lord ? The tree is recognized by its fruits, either of selfishness and bitterness, or of love and joy, which indicate their origin. Moreover, anyone who has had genuine experience of the divine dialogue knows that our Lord, when He speaks, has, if one may say so, a style of His own, which cannot be confused with any other. Finally we can, and often should, apply for some competent spiritual advice, and confront our "guidance" with the mind and tradition of the Church. The tradition (*paradosis*) is a sacred treasury in the eyes of the Orthodox Church. It must not be confounded with legend or with routine. It is a continuous line of thought and prayer, the way of the Apostles and the saints, a way from which we cannot deviate without danger. Far from constituting an external rule with which to comply mechanically, it is a living legacy which has to be freely received, organically assimi-lated, and faithfully transmitted. Tradition and personal guidance complete each other. St. Paul expressed it beautifully : "That good thing which was committed unto thee, keep by the Holy Ghost which dwelleth in us" (2 Tim. 1. 14). Tradition is the touchstone of our experiences of guidance, and helps us to interpret them rightly. On the other hand, each experience of guidance, however slight it may appear, enriches, deepens and renders more precise the tradition of the Church.

During the illuminative period, the direction of conscience exercised by a prudent and wise *pater pneumatikos* may be a great benefit. The spiritual father must however be careful of remaining only a "pedagogue unto Christ", *paidagogos eis Christon* (Gal. 3. 24). The soul must go beyond all human helpers, directly to the Light and Master within. To listen to Christ's speech in the soul, and to engage frequently in colloquy with Him, is of the utmost importance. A time must come when the soul will be able to repeat the words of the people of Sychar : " Now we believe, not because of thy saying : for we have heard him ourselves" (John 4. 42).

(7) *Praying to the Holy Ghost and Praying in the Holy Ghost*

The Orthodox Church has but few prayers directly addressed to the Holy Ghost. The chief expression of the Church's piety towards the Spirit is found in the *Pentekostarion* (the collection of services for the season of Pentecost). But there are two prayers, used at all seasons, which require our attention.

One opens most of the Orthodox services and corresponds after a fashion to the Latin *Veni Creator* :

"Heavenly King, Comforter, Spirit of truth, who art everywhere and fillest all, treasure of graces and giver of life, O come and dwell in us ; cleanse us from all defilement and save our souls, O gracious One."

The other prayer is :

"O Lord, who at the third hour, didst send down Thy most Holy Spirit upon Thine Apostles, do not take Him away from us, O Gracious One, but renew us who pray unto Thee."

We should like to quote also, though they are only a private prayer, the invocations of the Holy Spirit with which St. Symeon the New Theologian opens his *Divine Hymns of Love* :

"Come down, O true Light ! Come down, Life eternal. Come down, hidden mystery. Come down, ineffable treasure. . . . Come down, O constant rejoicing. Come down, Light that never fadeth. . . . Come down, Eternal Joy. Come down, Garland that never withereth. Come down, Thou whom my miserable soul ardently longs for and loves. Come down, Thou who art alone, to another, for I also am alone. . . . Come down, Thou who hast transformed Thyself into my desire . . ."

If there are few Orthodox prayers directly addressed to the Holy Spirit or concerning Him, we always can and must practise what St. Jude (20) calls "praying in the Holy Ghost." This means, either a prayer in which the words and the intentions are not our own, but are given by the Spirit, or a praying silence in which the soul unites herself to the unknown and continuous prayer of the Spirit. The Orthodox who use the "Jesus-prayer" are well acquainted with a kind of quiescence or latent presence of the Sacred Name of Jesus in the soul ; this state of "implicit prayer" signifies that the Holy Spirit has become the only and real Suppliant, the *solus Orans*, in ourselves. "The Spirit also helpeth our infirmities : for we know not what we should pray for as we ought ; but the Spirit itself maketh intercession for us with groanings which cannot be uttered" (Rom. 8. 26).

(8) *The Christ of the Spirit*

We have already asserted that the office of the Holy Ghost in the Christian life is to reveal and make present Jesus Christ to us. The Spirit unveils new aspects of our Lord. Christ, as disclosed by the Spirit after Pentecost, cannot be merely identified with the historical Jesus. "Though we have known Christ after the flesh, yet now henceforth know we Him no more" (2 Cor. 5. 16). Christ in glory and power, Christ whose Mystical Body is ever growing, the Christ of the Spirit, has replaced the Suffering Servant of Isaiah 53, though the bruises of the Servant remain eternally actual, offered and saving. Orthodox art, faithful to the traditions of primitive Basilican art, represents with predilection the transfigured, risen and glorified Christ, the enthroned and crowned King whom angels adore. In His members, Christ is mystically in agony. But the Head of the Body is the resplendent source of all light and strength.

To the Orthodox mind a "back-to-Jesus" movement, stripping the Gospel of all its supposed "later accretions", would not constitute progress. Real progress consists in becoming more and more deeply conscious of the presence and action of our Lord in all the phases of human life and of our own life. The "Galilean Gospel", the *ipsissima verba* of Jesus, cannot be isolated from the interpretations put upon it by the eye-witnesses of His Life and the ministers of His words. Modern criticism has made it perfectly clear that the Sermon on the Mount, taken by itself, does not provide an adequate explanation of the rise of Christianity. The vitalizing centre of Christian thought and devotion was neither a body of ethical teaching, simply relating the individual to his Father and Maker (Harnack, Tolstoi), nor a mere eschatological expectation (Schweitzer). Christianity was a stream of charismatic life flowing out with torrential might from Palestine upon the Greco-Roman world. It was a new spring-tide of the Spirit. Out of faith in, nay, out of experience of the risen and exalted Christ and the manifestation of His Glory grew the whole efflorescence of prayer and belief, of grace and self-giving, which we call the Holy Catholic Church. "Christ", on our lips, is no longer the exact equivalent of the name "Jesus" or of the Jewish title "Messiah". When we say "Christ", we think of the Pentecostal Christ, of the spiritual Lord of the new life. It is this spiritual Christ, and not merely the Christ of history, who was the source of Christianity. The confession of faith of the first Christian generation was : "Jesus is the Lord" (*Kyrios Christos*). But during the same period Paul wrote : "The Lord is the Spirit—*Kyrios to Pneuma*" (2 Cor. 3. 17). This equation magnificently expresses the fact that the Holy Spirit living in the Church is one with the historical Jesus, and is really the Spirit of Jesus (as well as the Spirit of the Father).

We have yet, perhaps, to recognize more clearly that the Spirit—or, if we prefer it, the Spiritual Christ (and by this phrase we do not mean to belittle in any way the distinct personality of the Holy Ghost)—is still a genuinely creative force among men to-day. Not only Paul but the author of the Book of Revelation, the Alexandrine exegetes, martyrs like Ignatius of Antioch, Felicitas, and Perpetua, and many others, have witnessed—(the "cloud of witnesses") —to the Spiritual Christ, to the actual charismatic presence of the Lord, as the great fact behind the whole Christian movement. Do *we* believe as intensely in the reality of the Spiritual Christ ? For the early Christians, the danger was of secluding themselves in the worshipping remembrance of the historical Jesus, and of perceiving but dimly the actuality of the Pentecostal Christ. For us, the danger is rather of localizing and limiting the Pentecostal Christ within the Apostolic or sub-Apostolic times, and so failing to acknowledge that He is *just as much present* now as He was then Men like Ignatius or Hermas would have admitted that a word of Jesus not recorded in the Gospels but received "through the Spirit" had as much claim to full authenticity and truth (though in another way) as a saying uttered in Capernaum or Jerusalem. We, in our day, should endeavour

to take the possibility of direct communications from the
Risen Lord most seriously, to become more vividly aware of
the absolute reality of His presence, to open our eyes and
ears more readily to the deeds and words of the Spiritual
Christ. The Christ of the Spirit is no figure of speech, no
mere symbol of a surviving influence; He is for ever alive
and present.

It is when we approach the Christ of the Spirit that we
realize best the "sonship" of Jesus. As Jesus was being
baptized in Jordan, "the Holy Ghost descended in a bodily
shape like a dove upon Him, and a voice came from heaven,
which said : Thou art my beloved Son ; in Thee I am well
pleased" (Luke 3. 22). When we see the Dove over
Christ, we hear the voice from heaven ; we begin to understand that the true life of Christ is hidden with the Father,
that this life of the Lord with the Father is something far
greater than His life with us, and that the acme of Christian
life is not reached until the soul, freeing herself from her
subjective pre-occupation, is admitted by grace into the
intimate relationship between the Father and the Son. In the
Son we learn to know the Father, who is, perhaps, remote and
vague in our eyes until then. We learn to share—so far as
our weakness can—the love of Jesus for His Father and His
consecration to Him. We become, in a new sense, the sons
of the Father. All this is achieved under the influence of the
Holy Ghost, for He is the link between Father and Son.
"Ye have received the spirit of adoption, whereby we cry,
Abba, Father. The Spirit itself beareth witness with our
spirit, that we are the children of God" (Rom. 8. 15, 16).
"And because ye are sons, God hath sent forth the Spirit of
his Son into your hearts, crying, Abba, Father" (Gal. 4. 6).

CHAPTER V

CHRIST OUR PASSOVER

(1) *The Paschal Lamb*

EUCHARISTIC GRACE FULFILS the grace of Baptism and the grace of Chrisma. We may call the grace of the Eucharist, "Easter grace", for "Christ our Passover is sacrificed for us" (1 Cor. 5. 7). In the Paschal mystery—the Holy of Holies—we find the three essential aspects or moments of the Eucharist : the Lord's Supper, the Passion and the Resurrection. Only a distorted piety can separate the Upper Room from Golgotha and the Sepulchre. The three sacred days—*triduum sacrum*, as the Latin liturgical books say—constitute an indivisible whole. There is but one Passover.

Side by side with the Fish and the Dove, the Christian art of the first centuries depicted the basket containing the Bread (sometimes the bread and the fish together) ; it also represented the bunch of grapes and, with special fondness, the Lamb. A mosaic of the sixth century represents the Lamb standing on a throne, at the foot of the Cross ; its side is pierced ; five streams of blood flow from its body. The Ewe feeds the Christians : the holy martyr Perpetua, in her dream, received from the Shepherd a mouthful of curdled milk. All the aspects of the Passover are indicated in these beautiful symbols.

(2) *The Supper of the Lamb*

"Blessed are they which are called unto the marriage-supper of the Lamb" (Rev. 19. 9). The *fractio panis*, the breaking of the bread, remains the centre of the holy mysteries. The Orthodox Church has always been reluctant to elaborate a theory explaining the Eucharist ; but her conception is definitely realistic. Whether "conversion", or "change" of the elements is postulated, whether, with Cyril of Jerusalem, the word *metabolē* is used, or, with Gregory of Nyssa, the word *metapoiesis*, or, with Chrysostom, the word *metarrythmesis*, the Orthodox Church does not mean a symbol, but a real Presence. St. John Chrysostom, the *doctor eucharisticus* of the Eastern Church, writes : "How many people say to-day : I would like to see Him, Himself, His face, His features, His clothes, His shoes ! Well, you see Him, you touch Him, you eat Him . . . He gives Himself to you." [1]

The Greek Fathers nevertheless eschewed the crude literalism which might become a kind of Eucharistic materialism. They warned us against a one-sided or disproportionate piety towards the sacramental action or elements. They knew that the Eucharistic Sacrament is not an end in itself, but a means to a spiritual reality greater than the Sacraments. Clement speaks of the incarnate Logos as of a "spiritual food" (*trophe pneumatike*). St. Basil says that the Christian eats the flesh of Christ and drinks His blood when he shares in the Logos, in His coming, in His teaching.[2] Origen writes that, beyond the Sacrament, there is a "deeper and more divine manner" of understanding the Eucharist : "This bread, which the God Logos calls His Body, is the Logos, fosterer of souls. . . . And this, which the God Logos calls His Blood, is the Logos who gives drink to men's hearts and splendidly inebriates them." [3] He writes again : "He who remembers that Christ our Passover has been sacrificed for us and that we must feast, eating the Flesh of the Word, at all times keepeth the Passover, passing ever in thought, word and deed from the things of this life

[1] *In Matt. hom.* LXXXII; *P.G.* LVIII, 743.
[2] *Epist.* VIII; *P.G.* XXXII, 253.
[3] *In Matt.* LXXXV; *P.G.* XIII, 1735.

to God, and hastening to His city." [1]   And St. Gregory
Nazianzen : "I shall offer a better sacrifice than those now
offered, inasmuch as truth is better than shadow" ; [2] he
elsewhere opposes the shadow (*skia*, *umbra*) to the true
food.

Communicating with Christ, we communicate with all His
members.   "For we being many are one bread and one body:
for we are partakers of that one bread" (1 Cor. 10. 13).   St.
John Damascene repeats the teaching of St. Paul, and reminds us that we are "concorporeal with Christ and members
of one another." [3]   The individual Jesus, the historical
Christ, was in some sense the *sacramentum*, the sign, of the
mystical Body and total Christ, who constitutes the *res*, the
full and ultimate reality of the Eucharist.

It is well known that Orthodox Christians communicate
far less frequently than Latins.   It is difficult to obtain an
exact idea of the practice of the majority of Greek Christians
in the times of St. Basil and St. John Chrysostom.   According to St. Basil [4] the faithful of the fourth century used to
communicate four times a week : on Sunday, Wednesday,
Friday and Saturday.   Basil advises them to communicate
every day.   On the days without a Eucharistic meeting
(*synaxis*), the faithful could communicate themselves
directly with the reserved Sacrament which they kept in
their houses.   On the other hand, St. John Chrysostom
states that many people used to communicate only once a
year.   He blames this neglect and recommends frequent
Communion.   In Russia the saintly Ignatius Briantchani-
nov (1867) and Father John of Kronstadt (908), as well as
many others, were defenders of frequent Communion.   A
more frequent participation of the modern Orthodox in the
Lord's Supper would certainly foster a closer intimacy with

[1] *Contr. Celsum*, VIII, 22.
[2] *Orat.* 26. 16.
[3] *De fide orthod.*, IV, 13.
[4] *Epist.* XCIII; *P.G.* XXXII, 484.

our Lord. The present practice of rather infrequent communions, prepared for each time by a few days of prayer
and retirement, has the advantage of aiding a serious preparation and increasing the respect for the Holy Mystery ;
it has the inconvenience of transforming into an exceptional
event what the most authorized Christian tradition considered as the blessed comfort of each day ; it also runs the
risk of mistaking for a kind of reward what is really a remedy
and a strength for the journey, *viaticum*. However, it would
be very contrary to the Orthodox mind to make the frequency
of our communions the criterion and measure of our personal approach to Christ. St. Augustine seems to have
given a profoundly wise judgment on the question, when
he said that both Zacchaeus and the centurion of Capernaum, through their different behaviour, equally honoured
the Lord in a divine manner, and that everyone ought to
act acccording to his own conscience.

The Orthodox Church emphasizes the fact that, in the
celebration of the Eucharist, our Lord Himself is the real
and invisible priest : "Thou Thyself both offerest and art
offered, Thou Thyself both dost receive and art distributed,
O Christ our God" says the text of the Liturgy. The
faithful take a most intimate share in the oblation. They
offer the *prosphorai*, small loaves of bread from which the
priest cuts out particles which are not consecrated, but are
put in the Chalice, after the communion, with what remains
of the precious Blood. These particles, every one of which
represents a particular Christian, either alive or dead, become
soaked into the sacred Blood ; they symbolize the union of
the Christians with the sacrifice of Christ. Every Eucharist
means the spiritual death—a mystical stab in the heart—of
all the participants and their fusion with Christ ; and every
one should become spiritually imbued with the Blood of
Our Lord.

It must be made quite clear that, in the Orthodox conception, the Holy Eucharist is not a *new* immolation of our Lord. Christ was immolated once for all. Our present Eucharists are offerings, actualizations, applications of this one all-sufficient Sacrifice. They are (we quote from the text of the Liturgy) a "sacrifice of praise", a "sacrifice in spirit" or "sacrifice in the Logos" ("logical sacrifice" *logike thusia*; "reasonable worship" would be inadequate to the idea involved). They are an "unbloody sacrifice". The Liturgy of St. Basil speaks of the "saving remembrance of the Passion" and says : "Presenting unto Thee the figures of the Holy Body and Blood of Thy Christ . . ." One should not conclude from this language that the Liturgy is mere symbolism. But the Orthodox tradition definitely excludes what we have called sacramental materialism. In the Holy Eucharist both the Presence and the Sacrifice of our Lord are real, but pneumatic and mystical. The text of our liturgies makes it equally clear that the Eucharist is the remembering, not only of the Death of our Lord, but of His Burial, Resurrection, and Ascension as well.

The Orthodox ritual of the Ordination of Priests shows that an everlasting link is established between the priesthood and the mystery of the Body and Blood of the Lord. The bishop places in the hand of the new priest a piece of the most Holy Bread and warns him to keep this deposit immaculate till the day of judgment, when he will have to answer for it.

(3) *The Blood of the Lamb*

The Lamb has obtained victory through His immolation. "In the midst of the throne . . . stood a Lamb as it had been slain" (Rev. 5. 6). The angels round about the throne say with a loud voice : "Worthy is the Lamb that was slain to receive power, and riches, and wisdom, and strength, and honour, and glory, and blessing" (Rev. 5. 12).

It has often been said that the Orthodox Church gives less consideration to the Cross of Christ than the Latin

Church does.   If this were true the Orthodox Church would betray the Gospel, for nobody can blot out the hard saying of our Lord : "If any man will come after me, let him deny himself, and take up his cross and follow me" (Matt. 16. 24).

But this allegation is untrue.   First it must be noticed that the worship of the Holy Cross, and therefore meditation on it, is more developed in the Orthodox than in the Latin ritual.   Not only has the Eastern Church, every year, three feasts of the Cross ; not only is the Cross abundantly mentioned during the services of the Passion Week ; but mention is made of it every day in the prayer of St. Basil which concludes the Sixth Hour and in the hymn to the Blessed Virgin said during the Ninth Hour.   Moreover, the Holy Cross is especially mentioned in the final or "dismissal" blessings of the services of each Wednesday and Friday.   At the end of every Eucharistic Liturgy, the faithful come and kiss the Cross.   The worship of the Cross may, of course, become so customary that there is a risk of forgetting its deep implications ; however, the theme of the Cross, being so often repeated, so strongly insisted upon, cannot be absent for long from the Orthodox mind.

It is true that the Eastern Church avoids realistic and bleeding representations of the crucified Lord.   Even crucified, He remains the Lord, *Kyrios*.   The Eastern pictures of the Cross, like those of the primitive basilicas, represent a crucified Christ, but a Christ crowned and glorified.   He remains, on His Cross, Christ the victorious, the conquering and triumphant, Christ the King, *Christus victor et rex*; His Passion is not merely a sacrificial suffering, but the glorious defeat of all evil.   The Orthodox Church does not separate the Cross from the Resurrection.   She says in her prayers : "We fall down before Thy Cross, O Lord, and we sing and glorify Thy Holy Resurrection."

This does not mean that the Orthodox Church fails to insist on our necessary union with the sufferings of Christ.

How could she forget the great teaching of Paul? "As the sufferings of Christ abound in us" (2 Cor. 1. 5); "We which live are always delivered unto death for Jesus' sake" (2 Cor. 4. 11); "I . . . rejoice in my sufferings . . . and fill up that which is behind of the afflictions of Christ in my flesh for his body's sake, which is the church" (Col. 1. 24). But the characteristic of the Eastern Church, in her attitude towards the Passion, is to approach it and to share in it with a certain exultation, with the feeling of an all-permeating joy and light. This was the attitude of Paul himself: "Always bearing about in the body the dying of the Lord Jesus, that the life also of Jesus might be made manifest in our body" (2 Cor. 4. 10); "O death, where is thy sting ? O grave, where is thy victory ?" (1. Cor. 15. 55). Were we to use Western analogies, we could say that the Orthodox approach to the sacred Wood is less related to the *Stabat Mater Dolorosa* and the Franciscan Passion-mysticism of the Middle Ages than to the triumphant world-wide famous hymn of Fortunatus : *Vexilla Regis prodeunt, fulget crucis mysterium. . . . Arbor decora et fulgida, ornata Regis purpura . . . Dicendo nationibus : regnavit a ligno Deus.*

This shade of meaning having been noted, we must assert that there are nevertheless to be found in the liturgical texts of the Orthodox Church accents which remind us of the modern Latin mystics. Chrysostom, Cyril of Alexandria, Epiphanios, the hymns of the *Oktoekos* and the *Paraklētikē*, speak in moving terms of the Side pierced by the lance. "Grant me to cling to Thy Side," says the hymn written by Romanus the "Singer" in honour of the Apostle Thomas. Nicholas Cabasilas sang and worshipped the depths of the "heart" of Jesus. The same Cabasilas wrote that in the Lord's Supper we appropriate "the holy wounds, the bruises and the death of Christ." St. Tikhon Zadonsky (1724-1783), who, perhaps more than any other Russian divine, was in continuity with the ancient Church Fathers, "had a vivid, almost palpable, feeling of the crucifixion" [1] and taught that "union in suffering leads to likeness in glory." Speaking of Russia, is there any literature which has approached the suffering Christ more humbly and lovingly than the Russian ?

One sees how unjustified is the assertion of the well-known contemporary Roman theologian Karl Adam, when he charges [2] the Orthodox Church with having fallen into monophysitism and lost the humanity of Christ. If such were the case, the Orthodox Church would not sing, in a *troparion* to the martyrs written by the "singers" Cyprian and Nicholas : "O Fathers, you have been wounded with love for Christ," and, in the *Meneai*, about a virgin-martyr : "Thee alone, my Saviour, I have loved."

The deep and passionate—though never mournful or abject—feeling of the Eastern Church towards the Cross is expressed in her attitude towards martyrdom. Origen's *Preparation to Martyrdom* may be recalled. Formerly the Church identified martyrdom with perfection, and considered the asceticism of monks and virgins a substitute for the effusion of blood. Can anyone who has read the fervent lines of St. Ignatius of Antioch, justly called *Theophoros* and *Christophoros*, ever forget them ? "Grant me nothing more than that I be poured out a libation to God, while there is still an altar ready . . . I am God's wheat, and I am ground by the teeth of wild beasts that I may be found pure bread of Christ. . . . Come, fire and cross and grapplings with wild beasts, cuttings and manglings, wrenching of bones, hacking of limbs, crushing of my whole body, come, cruel tortures of the devil to assail me. Only be it mine to attain unto Jesus Christ. . . . My *erōs* has been

---

[1] N. Gorodetzky, *The humiliated Christ in modern Russian thought* (London, 1938), p. 103.

[2] In *Christus unser Bruder* (Regensburg, 1930).

crucified, and there is no fire of material longing in me, but only a living water, saying within me : Come to the Father . . ." [1] To these early martyrs, first fruits of Christ, we should piously apply the words spoken by one of the Elders to the Seer : "These are they which came out of great tribulation, and have washed their robes, and made them white in the Blood of the Lamb" (Rev. 7. 14). We can say the same of the martyrs of the "great tribulation" of Bolshevism and of the "great tribulation" of the more recent German war.

In the Orthodox rite for the ordination of a bishop, the texts allude to the "true Shepherd who lays down His life for the sheep." The Shepherd-allegories of the Gospel are not mere idylls, but have a sacrificial undertone. Both the Shepherd and the Lamb immolate their life. The Ordination of every priest is a sharing in the sacrificial love of the Shepherd and the Lamb. The Lord Jesus celebrates an inner liturgy within the hearts of all His faithful, laymen and priests alike. A continuous sacrifice, of which Love is the high-priest, goes on : *Amor sacerdos immolat.*

Let us also remember that the Christian East has, more than the West, honoured evangelical non-resistance to violence. This is an aspect of communion with the Lamb ; "He is brought as a lamb to the slaughter, and as a sheep before her shearers is dumb, so he openeth not his mouth" (Isa. 53. 7). Russia comemmorates with special affection, as martyrs, the young princes Boris and Gleb who were, in the beginnings of Russian history, the willing victims of a murder. Origen proclaimed : "We do not serve as soldiers, even though the Emperor require it." [2] The Eastern canons, known as the Egyptian Church Order, ruled : "If a catechumen or a believer wishes to become a soldier let him be rejected for he has despised God." [3] As late as

---

[1] *Ad Roman.*   [2] *Contra Cals.* VIII, 73.
[3] Ed Funk, XI, 11.

the fourth century, when the West had gradually accepted
the idea of a "just" war and the legitimacy of military
service, St. Basil the Great taught that they who had shed
blood in war should abstain from communion for three
years.[1]

The present attitude of Church officials, Eastern and
Western alike, who condone war, cannot alter the fact that
the most ancient tradition of the Church tends in the opposite
direction. The West, since the Council of Arles (314) and
the writings of Ambrose and chiefly Augustine, was (with
the notable exception of strict anti-militarists like St. Martin
of Tours, who, although he was a soldier, refused to fight,
and St. Paulinus of Nola) far more instrumental than the
East in bringing about that change of mind.

(4) *The Marriage of the Lamb*

"Let us be glad and rejoice, and give honour to him : for
the marriage of the Lamb is come . . ." (Rev. 19. 7).
This expression, the "marriage of the Lamb", may strike us
as strange. What is that wedding ? "Come hither, I will
shew thee the bride, the Lamb's wife" (Rev. 21. 9).

It is the "great city, the holy Jerusalem,"—the Church of
Christ—which was shown to the Seer of the Book of Revelation as the Bride of the Lamb. A constant Christian
tradition has nevertheless applied the nuptial analogies to
the relationship between the Lord Jesus and individual
souls.

We have already mentioned the special nearness of the
virgins to the Lamb, whom they follow "whithersoever he
goeth" (Rev. 14. 4). Both martyrs and virgins stand close
to the Lord. There exists a link between these two categories. St. Methodius writes : "The virgins bind themselves to a kind of perpetual martyrdom." If they break
their promise, they become "adulterous towards the

[1] *P.G.* XXXII, 681.

Saviour." East and West meet here, in the idea of a wedding between Christ and the virgins.

The Eastern Church has entered quite as much as the Western Church into nuptial mysticism. It is often asserted that the nuptial symbols are peculiar to the Latins and alien to the spirit of Orthodoxy, but an objective consideration of the matter belies such a view. The Eastern and Western outward forms of the nuptial mysticism may be at variance ; the monastic profession of women, for instance, does not assume in the East as it does in the West the externals of a wedding. The fundamental idea is nevertheless the same. This nuptial mysticism has most ancient and deep roots. The words of the Lord, "I will betroth thee unto Me for ever" (Hos. 2. 19), sum up the whole book of Hosea. Origen, by writing his two homilies on the Song of Songs, set Christian spirituality on a way of which the Church approved. A *troparion* to St. Macrina speaks of the divine Husband who introduces her into the "nuptial chamber". We read in St. Methodius : "I keep myself pure for Thee, my Bridegroom, and with a flaming torch come forth to meet Thee." [1] Every night, in the service of the *mesonyktion*, the Orthodox Church sings : "Here comes the Bridegroom . . . Let Christ grant thee entrance into the divine nuptial chamber." The Orthodox Church has no experience of the realistic visions which, in the minds of certain Latin mystics, accompany the idea of mystical marriage (exchange of rings, etc.), but she undoubtedly acknowledges mystical marriage as a reality and a very high plane of spiritual life. This is the marriage of the Lamb.

We have already spoken of human marriages and insisted on the fact that the Church sets virginity (or celibacy for Christ's sake) higher. But we must do full justice to the splendid vision which the Church forms of the true union of man and woman. Marriage in the full Christian sense—

[1] *Symposium*, XI, 2.

that is, marriage in Christ—is a sharing in the marriage between the Lamb and the Church. The ritual of Orthodox marriage includes the reading of St. Paul's words : "The husband is the head of the wife, even as Christ is the head of the church : and he is the saviour of the body. . . . Husbands, love your wives, even as Christ also loved the church, and gave himself for it . . . They two shall be one flesh. This is a great mystery : but I speak concerning Christ and the Church" (Eph. 5. 23, 25, 31, 32). The Orthodox Church moreover established a link between marriage and martyrdom. She invokes, in the wedding service, the holy martyrs, and especially the great martyr Procopius, who is said to have exhorted twelve women to go to martyrdom as to marriage ; she also invokes, in the same service, St. Helen, who is believed to have discovered the wood of the Holy Cross. She crowns the new husband and wife (the rite of the *stephanōsis*) : this is a survival not of the pagan coronation of spouses as a sign of joy, but of the early Christian symbolism according to which the crown meant martyrdom. Although reasons of locality, rather than the idea of martyrdom, may, in Palestine, have led to the mention of St. Procopius, there is no doubt that the Orthodox Church wants to impress on the minds of the husband and wife that marriage requires a self-sacrifice, a self-immolation almost equal to martyrdom.

Both virginity and marriage (when this last is entirely what it ought to be) thus participate in the grace of the Lamb, in the Eucharistic and Paschal grace. A thorough application of this idea—perhaps mistaken, perhaps prophetical, but in any case deeply sincere—was manifested in the life of the great Russian theologian Bukharev (the Archimandrite Theodore, 1822–1871). His teaching and writings and, later on, his voluntary reduction to the lay-state and his wedding, illustrate a "kenotic will" to go to the world as a sinner under penance, to reveal the Lamb (his favourite theme of meditation) to all classes of the world, and to reflect in every condition of his existence Christ's union with his church.

(5) *The Triumph of the Lamb*

Christ immolated is also the risen Christ. It has often been said (so often that it has almost become a commonplace) that the joy of Easter is a special characteristic of the Orthodox Church. If the liturgical texts only are considered, the Latin *praeconium paschale* expresses no less paschal exultation than the Orthodox service. Nevertheless the peculiar Orthodox attitude towards the Grave of Christ must be noticed and explained.

It seems that, to the Orthodox, the Sepulchre of our Lord is an instrument of salvation, as the Cross is to Western Christians. The Orthodox by no means belittle the saving value of the Cross ; but they have an original approach to the Sepulchre ; they even give to the empty Tomb, as the symbol of the Resurrection, a kind of predominance over the Cross—an attitude which, we think, is less frequently found in the West. The Basilica of the Holy Sepulchre in Jerusalem includes the traditional sites of both the Crucifixion and the Resurrection, and it is worth noticing that the centre of the Basilica and of its worship is not Golgotha, but the place of the Resurrection (the *anastasis*). Nothing can give a better idea of the Orthodox paschal attitude than to see the faithful kneeling in front of the *anastasis*, stooping in order to enter the tomb, and kissing with tears the rock of the sacred Grave.

The Orthodox liturgical texts speak of the Lord's Sepulchre as being the "source of life". In the homily of St. John Chrysostom which is always read during the Easter service, it is said that "pardon hath shone forth from the grave". Certain words of this homily—"Rejoice to-day, both ye who have fasted and ye who have disregarded the fast"—are apparently inconsistent with the Western conception, according to which the joy of the Resurrection can be approached only through the immolation of Golgotha. But we must not forget that the Apostles were graciously admitted to the joy of the Resurrection without having shared in the immolation of the Lord. They had, indeed, fled from it. They knew later on, through their own martyrdom, the meaning of the Cross. But it may be affirmed that, if they became able to give their lives for Christ, it was because the strength of the Resurrection had first been communicated to them. In the same manner the Orthodox Church seems to suggest that the sinner cannot experience the Cross if he has not received first the splendour and the strength of the risen Christ. Dying with Christ remains the necessary prerequisite for rising with Him, but the "dying with" and the "rising with" will always be out of our reach if the Presence of the risen Lord and the victorious grace of His Sepulchre are not set before us as a free gift, prior to any sacrificial decision on our part. Hence this condescension of the Orthodox Church at Easter towards all sinners, and this gratuitous offer of the Paschal gift even to those who are not prepared for it. If only they open their hearts to the joy of the Resurrection, the right preparation—"infused", not "acquired", we might say, in the language of mystical theology—is immediately imparted to them and they will become able to share both in the Cross and in the glorified Grave of the Lord, His Passion and Resurrection.

There is here a certain difference of attitude between East and West. Both acknowledge the indissoluble correlation of Good Friday and Easter Sunday, but the respective order of these two days is conceived differently.

The joy of the Resurrection is not limited to Easter. In each Liturgy, after the communion, the deacon says a hymn in which the themes of the Cross and the Sepulchre are mingled : "We have seen the Resurrection of Christ ;

let us worship the Lord Jesus . . . Thy Cross, O Christ, we adore ; we sing and glorify Thy Holy Resurrection . . . We bless the Lord and of His Resurrection we sing ; for He hath endured the Cross . . . O Thou great Passover hallowed above all, O Christ ! '' This connection and balance of the two themes exactly expresses the Orthodox view.

It should also be noticed that, in the symbolism of the Orthodox Churches, the altar represents the Holy Sepulchre, while Golgotha is rather signified by the table (*proskomedia* or *prothesis*) on which the bread and wine are prepared and disposed till they are solemnly conveyed to the altar.

The notion of Resurrection leads us to another idea on which recent Orthodox writers, mainly Russian, have laid much emphasis : the idea of the Transfiguration.

The exalted view which modern Russian piety takes of the Transfiguration is not quite identical with the ancient traditional interpretation. For many Orthodox, the Transfiguration of Our Lord announces and symbolizes the metamorphosis of this world into a new world. It is a somewhat eschatological view, foreshadowed in the transformation of water into wine at Cana. (Readers of Dostoievsky will remember the beautiful chapter "Cana of Galilee" in *The Brothers Karamasov*.) This conception of the Transfiguration as a cosmical event, an eschatological renewing, contains a deep truth ; it coincides with many Scriptural texts ; it fits in with the optimistic expectations of many Greek Fathers and specially the views of St. Gregory of Nyssa about the "universal restoration" (*apokatastasis*). Nevertheless patristic tradition restricts the use of the word "Transfiguration" to the event described by the Gospels, and the evangelical text makes it clear that this event was an experience immediately related to the Person of our Lord. It was the answer to the great confession of Peter—a Messianic revelation. Jesus was "glorified" : the "glory" of the Father in the Hebrew as well as Greek sense of a physical phenomenon, of the divine luminous effulgence, came upon Him. A similar "glorification" of Jesus in our own experience may constitute the practical application of the Transfiguration to our spiritual life. The hesychasts thought that a physical experience was possible in our case, just as in the case of the Apostles, and that the perception of the "light of Tabor" is the goal of Christian contemplation. We believe that this has happened and may happen. But, in the absence of the objective, external light of the Transfiguration, we can inwardly and invisibly experience, through grace, a spiritual transfiguration of Christ. There are times when we become aware, in a sudden and overwhelming manner, that this Jesus "Whom having not seen, ye love ; in whom, though now ye see Him not, yet believing . . ." (1 Peter 1. 8) is the Lord and the Son. He, within our souls, appears as clothed with splendour and strength. We feel enraptured and overflowing with joy. At such times we hardly think of a transfiguration of the world. It is enough for us to be made conscious of the Lordship and Sonship of our Master, to obtain an inward glimpse of the radiance of the Godhead in Him. What more could we desire ? And, when such an experience is the lot of genuine mystics, they would add : what more could we sustain ? Yet the whole creation is called to be penetrated through and through by the "glory" of God.

The Orthodox emphasis on the Transfiguration is connected with two other notions particularly important in Greek thought : deification and vision, *theōsis* and *opsis*.

Deification, as we have already said, is considered by the Greek Fathers to be the crown of spiritual life, the normal goal of human destiny. "Let us become God because of Him, since He became man because of us" says St. Gregory Nazianzen.[1] This deification—in which the human essence is not modified but henceforth exists by the imme-

---

[1] *Orat.* I. 5.

diate virtue and immediate support of the Divine Being, just as, in the Incarnation, the human nature of Christ does not "subsist in itself", but is assumed and supported by His Divine nature—is synonymous with the "full union" in the technical language of the Western mystics. Vladimir Soloviev writes :

"Your tendencies and ambitions come from God. They are remote calls from His kindness . . . If you wish to be upraised unto God, if you wish to be so united with God, that God is all in you, if you despair because, eager to share in the divine nature, you have a glimpse of it in its inaccessible infinity, then, take assurance. The Father, the Son, and the Holy Spirit are calling you, indeed, to ascend unto Them.

"They are ready to come down towards you and in you, in order to live as the habitual guests of your soul. They promise to your whole being, in exchange for what is good in it, a transformation, at first mysterious and invisible, but soon resplendent and glorious, a union and assimilation that will divinize you." [1]

Deification may be a constant and progressive union. It may also be very intermittent and interrupted by falls. It is not, for the Christian, something extraordinary, but the quite ordinary development and stabilization of the state which man is called to experience after baptism, after Chrismation, after Eucharistic Communion, and, generally, whenever he adheres to God with his whole heart and with his whole mind. Deification, therefore, is something much simpler and more frequent than is often thought. It admits of various degrees, which represent the growth of Christ in us. The perfect deification of a man is reached when Christ has attained in him the stature allowed by God to the capacity of that man : "One star differeth from another star in glory" (1 Cor. 15. 41) ; "Till we all come . . . unto the measure of the stature of the fulness of

[1] Soloviev, *Lectures on Theandrism*.

Christ" (Eph. 4. 13). The fulness of Christ is given only to the Mystical Body as a whole.

The process of deification cannot be considered apart from the Person of Christ. It is not a metaphysical, a neo-Platonic, deification. It is operated through the Sacred Humanity of our Lord. The incarnate Christ remains the Alpha and the Omega of our spiritual life. Therefore, true as is the idea of deification, dear as it is to the Greek Fathers, we find the mystical union still more warmly, and more vividly, represented in the words of Holy Scripture itself : "Abide in me, and I in you. . . . I am the vine, ye are the branches"; "I in them, and thou in me, that they may be perfect in one" (John 15. 4, 5; 17. 23). "My beloved is mine, and I am his" (Song of Songs 2. 16).

Unitive life is not necessarily accompanied by ecstasies or visions. The history of spirituality shows, however, such a close link between mystical union and vision that it may be beneficial to lay some stress on this last element. We shall not dwell on the psycho-physiological description of the visions of the mystics. We would, rather, outline the theological background of the concept of "vision".

Under that name, we should not merely (and narrowly) understand perceptions of our eyes directly produced by God, without adequate external and material causes. We should give to the word "vision" a very wide meaning. There are objective sensory visions. There are also purely inner or intellectual visions. A divine vision may be devoid of any precise image. It may be the vague and diffuse feeling of an outward or inner light, the awareness of an atmosphere, the becoming conscious of a Presence. It may be the apprehension of a goal given to our will, and of a divine line of direction. It may even be the obscure apprehension of a shapeless and unutterable essence. It may be a prophetic dream. Vision is a ladder with numerous rungs. But all these forms are a participation, more or less precise, of the heavenly vision that is kept in store for us : "As it is written," says St. Paul, "eye hath not seen, nor ear heard, neither have entered into the heart of man, the things which God hath prepared for them that love him" (1 Cor. 2. 9). St. John says : "It doth not yet appear what we shall be: but we know that, when He shall appear, we shall be like Him ; for we shall see Him as He is" (1 John 3. 2).

We could therefore define every vision granted to us on earth as an anticipation and reflection, however dim, of the vision of God in heaven. Generally speaking, there is an ascending gradation in the external phenomena of the spiritual life. This gradation begins with "words" and finishes with "vision". At first one listens to God, at the end one sees Him.

Divine locutions and visions may coincide, but the gift of sight represents a somewhat high level. The vision is a kind of climax. It is true that many visions have been imparted to the saints and prophets. Spiritual giants like Moses and Paul even obtained some special vision of God which the tradition of the Church has placed above all others : "I will come to visions and revelations of the Lord. I knew a man in Christ . . . such an one caught up to the third heaven . . . and heard unspeakable words, which it is not lawful for a man to utter" (2 Cor. 12. 1–4). But St. Paul adds—and his voice is here the voice of all the genuine mystics of the whole Church : "Yet of myself I will not glory, but in mine infirmities" (2 Cor. 12. 5).

If every vision is a foretaste of heaven, it is already a participation in angelic life. We reach here the hidden, loving link which exists between the Angels and the contemplatives. We have already seen how, in the Orthodox Church, the first monastic profession is a kind of new baptism. The second monastic profession, by which a monk is set apart for uninterrupted prayer and contemplation, is called "taking the great and angelic habit". The monk thus dedicated to the "angelic life" should normally reach the highest mystical achievements accessible to a Christian. On the new habit received by the monk who enters the way of the Angels, the instruments of the Passion of Our Lord are represented. This illustrates the closeness of these two themes : the divine passion and the divine Vision. Passion, Resurrection, Contemplation, Transfiguration, Eucharist, Vision— these are so many aspects of the same Paschal grace, of the Lord's Passover.

We cannot speak of vision without coming to the theme of the Light. This theme is most important. All the mysticism of the Old Testament is centred around the *Shekinah*, the dwelling of God among men, the abiding Presence. The Shekinah was visibly manifested under the form of a light, the divine "glory" (in the Burning Bush, on Sinai, over the Tabernacle, etc.). In the New Testament the ideas of "glory" and "glorification" often recur, and they must be understood, not in a merely moral sense, but in reference to the divine, and eventually visible, light. "God is light" writes St. John (1 John 1. 5). "I am the light of the world" says Jesus (John 8. 12). Our Paschal Lamb is associated with the light : "The city had no need of the sun . . . for the glory of God did lighten it, and the Lamb is the light thereof" (Rev. 21. 23). A profound sentence of St. Paul explains at the same time the meaning of the Transfiguration and the inner process of "glorification" of the Lord Jesus in ourselves : "God, who commanded the light to shine out of darkness, hath shined in our hearts, to give the light of the knowledge of the glory of God in the face of Jesus Christ" (2 Cor. 4. 6). Paul himself, when he met the Lord on the road to Damascus, was suddenly surrounded by the splendour of a light from Heaven (Acts 9. 3). A careful examination of all the New Testament references to the "light" and the "glory" would show what place these notions held in the mysticism of the Christians of the first generation. The Greeks received them from the Jews. They had a natural inclination towards the "luminous". Hence the centrality of the Transfiguration, of the notions of *phōs* and *doxa*, light and glory, in the mysticism of the Orthodox Church. Hence the emphasis of hesychasm on the vision of the light of Tabor. This emphasis on the luminous is perhaps what most strikingly differentiates the Christian East from the Christian West. The Eucharist itself is, in the Orthodox conception, a manifestation of the divine Light. The Choir sings after the Communion : "We have seen the true Light." Every evening, at sunset, the Orthodox Church sings the beautiful and most ancient hymn *Phōs hilaron hagias doxēs*, "Gladsome Light of the holy Glory. . . ." For Hellenic Christianity Jesus is, perhaps more than anything else, *Kyrios tēs doxēs*, the "Lord of Glory" (James 2. 1).

What is the connection between this Light-mysticism and the mysticism of Love ? The same Apostle who wrote that "God is light" said also "God is Love" (1 John 4. 8). Throughout our journey the Lord Jesus is asking us the same question which grieved Peter : "Lovest thou Me ?" Love strives towards vision. Love lives in an atmosphere of light. Mary of Magdala near the tomb, and Peter, James, and John on the mountain, were privileged seers because they loved more.

Every vision is a Paschal vision, a vision of the risen Christ. Our Lord remains the centre of the visions of the Christian mystics, but the Father and the Spirit also operate in every vision. St. Basil expressed this truth in a marvellous synthesis ; he said that the Holy Ghost, by His light, will show us God in the Logos.[1] This is also what is indicated by the inspired words : "In Thy Light shall we see Light" (Ps. 36. 9).

Eternal life will bring the fulness of vision, "For now we

[1] *De Spir. Sanct.* XVII, 4 ; *P.G.* XXXIV, 154.

see through a glass, darkly ; but then face to face : now I know in part; but then I shall know even as also I am known" (1 Cor. 13. 12). But, in this earthly life, every Christian, whoever he may be, can obtain at least a glimpse of the Vision. Some ray from the glory of God may be granted to him. These glimpses, these rays, are often given; far more often than we think. And it is only because of these gracious gifts that many who are heavily laden are able to live on. The Face of our Lord can be dimly reflected in the mirror of the heart of man. If the Lord Jesus calls us and says : "What will ye that I shall do unto you? " let us answer : "Lord, that our eyes may be opened" (Matt. 20. 32 ff.). For a vision is destined to every man. And blessed are they who, at the journey's end, can say : "I was not disobedient unto the heavenly vision" (Acts 26. 19).

APPENDIX

THIRTY YEARS have elapsed since the publication of the preceding pages. Readers may still find in them a clear and objective presentation of what one might call traditional Orthodoxy, though they are imperfect and incomplete. But, since then, much has been written on this topic ; many questions have been considered in a new way. So it may not be altogether unnecessary to complete the former book, as far as possible.

Russian emigration has remained the most important, if not the sole, means of spreading Orthodox piety in the West. It brought in the seeds and the first fruits of the movement of religious renewal which took place in Russia at the beginning of this century—the influence of some modern ascetics; devotion to John of Kronstadt and St. Seraphim of Sarov ; the new interest taken in ikons ; the "sophiology" derived from Soloviev, developed by P. Florensky (a confessor of the Faith) in a brilliant book, of an affected stylization, aestheticism and apparently omniscient versatility, and also by the Marxist converted to Christianity, Bulgakov. There was also the conjunction of new theological trends with Russian symbolist poetry (A. Blok and others) ; one should also take into account certain tendencies of doubtful value, in which were mingled a questionable mysticism, eroticism and occultism (Merejkovsky, Hippius, Rozanov). All these paths crossed one another.[1] The names of Dostoievsky, of Bulgakov and Berdyaev are those which come to mind most easily when one dwells on the spiritual atmosphere of the earliest Russian emigrants. Many Russians, and, misled by them, many Westerners, have seen in these men three representatives of Orthodox spirituality. In fact none of these three, whose talent was unmistakable, was such. Dostoievsky can move us deeply, but neither his private life, nor his excessive nationalism, nor his hatred for the Jews, nor his cultus of the Mother Earth, corresponds with the Gospel of Christ ; and the monks of Optina refused to reckon as "theirs" Aliocha Karamazov and his spiritual father, Zossima, however attractive they may have been. Bulgakov was by no means the heretic that his enemies accused him of being,[2] but his speculations about wisdom remained very personal and foreign to the traditional teaching of the Orthodox Church.

As for Berdyaev, he never claimed to represent Orthodoxy. Champion of human liberty above all else, he never expressed that radical obedience to the will of God which was found in Jesus, nor the deep humility characteristic of the saints of the Orthodox Church. This must be said without failing to recognize the nobility and generosity of his nature.

In the next generation, V. Lossky attempted to make a synthesis of the spirituality of the Eastern Church. His views on negative or "apophatic" theology, on the Name, the image, the ikon, the divine vision, expressed with understanding and clarity, have aroused the interest and acceptance of many in the West. Important reservations may and indeed must be made concerning some of his views, but Lossky's deep piety and his gift for friendship must also be mentioned.[3]

Lossky's contemporary, P. Evdokimov, may be said to have opened up to the West a new vision of marriage, the "sacrament of love". Drawing his inspiration from Boukharev, who had asked to be demoted from the priesthood in order to marry and undergo the experience of both monastic and conjugal life in Christ, Evdokimov spoke of an "interiorised monasticism", a profound vision, which yet incurs the risk of minimizing the solemn consecration which the Church confers on the monk. Evdokimov's spirituality is at one and the same time very respectful of tradition and deeply influenced by modern existentialism. His work is actively carried on in France by O. Clement.[4]

The younger theological Orthodox generation seems to avoid the above-mentioned trends and to concentrate, especially in America, upon a more rigorous Orthodoxy, more dogmatic, more patristic, more deeply inspired by Gregory Palamas. Side by side with Palamism, hesychasm and the "prayer of Jesus" are developing in a remarkable way. There may be some danger that the symbol may ultimately replace the reality, or at least veil it, and that the invocation of the Name may in some cases prove an obstacle to the complete liberation when the Name itself should disappear before the invisible and inexpressible Presence.[5]

A simple and modest "evangelical Orthodox spirituality" is set before us in the life of St. Tikhon, bishop of Zadonsk, whose life has been written by N. Gorodetzsky. This evangelical and patristic-based Orthodoxy can take the form of heroic devotedness to the poor and those in distress. Mother Maria Skobtsova practised that form of asceticism in Paris and, during the second world war, she gave her life for others in a German extermination camp. Her name is a symbol.

The development of Orthodox spirituality in Orthodox Churches outside Russia deserves full attention. In Romanian monasteries, as elsewhere, a great development of hesychasm is taking place. Greece has recently given rise to great spiritual figures, such as Silouan on Mount Athos and Amphilochios on Patmos. The religious revival brought about by the Zoe confraternity in Greece is well known. Following on political vicissitudes, the work of Zoe has been brought to an end. Its enemies rejoiced over this.[6] The immediate future will show whether they can manage to do better.

There is no dividing wall between spirituality and ethics. Among many Orthodox one notices a divorce between high spiritual aspirations (or theological speculations) and consciousness of present duty. People willingly admit that they are "guilty of everything, towards everybody", thus avoiding the necessity for facing oneself as one is, and of laying bare before God such or such open wound of the sinful soul. The notions of sin, repentance, redemption, fade away in a vague notion of "incarnationism". One should give a real and living sense to the word "conversion".

There are two special points on which the Orthodox might wish their Church to give more precise directions. Many of them suffer because it speaks so seldom about justice, whether social, economic, political or international. The Orthodox Church is too often silent concerning human rights, freedom, the dignity of human beings. (Besides, she herself persecuted others and provoked persecution when she had the power to do so.) Ecumenical organizations dare not speak of human rights, of liberty, human dignity, for fear of embarrassing the Churches practically enslaved by totalitarian States; and some dignitaries of these Churches would like ecumenism to be limited to the easier field of pure theology.

Another aspect on which the Orthodox Church is behindhand, compared with other Churches, is in the sexual field. While other Churches, including Rome, work at "re-thinking" in depth, in the light of biology, psychology, pastoral considerations, such questions as the true finality and validity of marriage, extra-conjugal relations, auto-eroticism, homosexuality, the Orthodox Church seems to act as though these problems did not exist or could be solved by the same outlook and means as in past centuries. "Jesus Christ is the same, yesterday and today", but the field and the possibilities of his love and his grace are always open to further exploration.

The participation of Orthodox Churches in the World Council of Churches does not appear to have led to any influencing of Orthodox spirituality by non-Orthodox views, except in the case of a few professional theologians. Devotion to St. Theresa of the Child Jesus and the pilgrimage of La Salette[7] have aroused moments of fervour among Russian emigrés in France, but that is already past history. The great Protestant voices of Barth and Schweitzer have scarcely been heard by Orthodox ears. A small number of Orthodox have joined the Oxford Groups or Moral Rearmament, or have worked with them, but these are exceptions. The great majority of Orthodox, even if they have had "personal ecumenical contacts", have not entered by a living experience into the deep emotions of Protestant consciences: the Lutheran emotion of salvation through faith, the Calvinist awareness of "the glory of God", the Baptist and Methodist emotion of conversion, the Quaker emotion of "the inner light" and of purely silent worship. On the other hand, Orthodox spirituality has had considerable influence in non-Orthodox circles, especially in England. At first restricted to the Anglican "High Church" tendency and Anglo-Catholicism, Orthodox influence has grown and reached a considerable number of people.[8] The practice of the "prayer of Jesus" has found adherents in unexpected groups. In America it was "discovered" by young people, who try to experiment with it as they experiment with drugs and with Zen Buddhism. Together with a frequently sincere desire, there is to be found a fashionable pursuit and a danger.

We all know that among Roman Catholics and Protestants alike the idea of liturgical reform has recently been associated with that of an "updating" of the Church. As Orthodox piety is very largely liturgical piety, is the same idea present there? It does not appear that, on the whole, the Orthodox faithful are asking for fundamental changes in their forms of worship. Of course, some improvements are possible and desirable: some abbreviations, simplifications, a return to older and purer forms of singing, a more active participation of the faithful, a deeper consciousness of the relationship between eucharistic communion and the fact of belonging to a loved community, the realization that the Liturgy is Pentecost as well as Easter, a greater attention paid to the ministry of the Word. But all these points are to be found in the Liturgy of St. John Chrysostom, the most frequently used. It could be said that this Liturgy constitutes the most exact and measured expression of the main elements of Orthodoxy. It is the bond linking together and uniting the main strands of Orthodox spirituality.

It is impossible to separate liturgical questions from those concerning ikons. We are witnessing a real revival of ikons.[9] A revival in a three-fold sense: people are writing more than ever before about the theological significance and the history of ikons; they seek out and appreciate authentic ikons; and new ones are being painted in the spirit of primitive tradition and are far removed from the mediocrity and insipidity of some outdated forms of religious pictures. This new valuation of the ikon rests to a certain extent on fashion and commercial interests. But easily counter-balancing these dangers is the fact that the ikon may greatly help our approach to that single Ikon, not man-made but painted within us by the Holy Spirit, of which each ecclesiastical ikon is but an aspect and a reflection. Modern abstract art could help to introduce us into the world of the ikon.

The Pentecostal movement, which has developed so successfully in Protestant Churches, and which finds many followers also in the Roman Catholic Church, has not yet had much influence in Orthodox circles. It has however influenced these in Paris, England, and especially in America,[10] less in the shape of healings and "speaking in tongues" than in charismatic movements devoted to prayer and silent meditation. Such activities take place outside the main Orthodox forms of worship, but without opposition to or separation from the Orthodox Church.

Among the different streams of Orthodox spirituality, we must discern a certain type of Orthodox piety, which is neither the frequently intellectualist piety of the Greeks, nor the heart-rending devotion of the Slavs. This is the spirituality of the Arabic-speaking Orthodox, that of Palestine, Syria, Lebanon and other Middle-Eastern countries. Even during the first Christian centuries the spirituality of Antioch, sober, scriptural, evangelical, practical, in a word, the piety of St. John Chrysostom, differed from the speculative piety of Alexandria and Constantinople. We find these same characteristics, clearly marked, in the Arabic-speaking Orthodox piety of today. More than any other Orthodox Church, the Arab

Orthodox Church is turning towards practical problems and bases itself on the gospel.   Under the dominant influence of the Orthodox Youth Movement of the Middle East (notably that of Metropolitan Georges Khodre), Arab Orthodoxy seeks to define "Arabism" in religious terms, to deepen its understanding of the promises made by God to Hagar, to Ishmael, to the Arab nation, and to take towards Israel an attitude favouring "Palestinian man", who has become a symbol of liberation.   The problems of social justice, of violence and non-violence, of collaboration between Orthodox Christians and pro-Marxist revolutionaries, of help to the *fedayin*, are becoming problems of the first order.

A powerful movement of mutual understanding between Orthodox Christians and Muslims is developing (school of L. Massignon, Gardet, Anawati, Moubarrack and Hayek).   It is noteworthy that the first Lenten sermon preached in 1975 in the Latin cathedral of Beirut was given by the Imam Mussa Sadr, leader of the Shiite Muslims in Lebanon.   A renewal of monastic life, for both men and women, is taking place in the Lebanese mountains, and Pentecostalism is finding many young recruits in Beirut.

Recent theological views expressed in such phrases as "The Death of God", "Non-religious Christianity", "God as the ultimate concern" and in the book *Honest to God* have found scant opening and sympathy in Orthodox centres.   That is not because the works of Tillich, Bonhoeffer, Robinson and many others do not contain stimulating and valuable elements.   But most Orthodox believers consider that the simple faith expressed in the Nicene Creed and the Liturgy of St. John Chrysostom still remains a common, not outdated cement, and that from ancient sources new strength may still come.[11]

We might wonder what has become of interior Orthodox piety in some countries situated beyond the Iron Curtain.   We know that solemn pontifical liturgies continue to take place ; that ecclesiastical authorities still maintain that there is no persecution ; that, from time to time, some illustrious "protesters", generally belonging to the world of literature, manage to cross the frontier and, once safely abroad, vehemently denounce the anti-religious persecution.   Sometimes they even attack it from within the country.   (One might wonder why, in these spectacular denunciations, we see no sign of an attitude of forgiveness and pardon towards the persecutors.)

What we do not know, is how and how much the condition of an Orthodox Christian suffering for his faith can, no longer in exterior ritual manifestations, but in the soul's most intimate sanctuary, create a new climate, a special one, open to ways hitherto unperceived and unexplored. We should like to know more about what is taking place in silence among the masses of lowly men and women who believe, who pray, who suffer.

It is not impossible that the restrictive measures taken against religious belief by the totalitarian States may lead Orthodox piety to a considerable renewal.   During the second world war we saw the growth of a typical spirituality in concentration camps where many barriers disappeared and where beyond denominations and labels was wrought a deep union of souls before and in the same Lord. The hour may be coming when, as in the first centuries, the state of persecution will become the normal state of the disciples of Jesus. Through martyrdom, torture and prison will appear more clearly, in its purity and fire, worship in spirit and in truth.

NOTES

[1] N. Zernov's book, *The Russian Religious Renaissance of the Twentieth Century* (London, 1963), gives the most detailed and accurate description of this intellectual panorama.

[2] Bulgakov did not teach that Divine Wisdom (Sophia) was a fourth hypostasis (person) of the Trinity, but that it is a hypostasibility, an infinite possibility of a created personalization of an uncreated divine energy.

[3] It would be a fair objection to Lossky's views to state that there is not *one* mystical theology of the Eastern Church, but that there are several Eastern Churches (Armenian, Coptic, etc.) and, within each one, different mystical currents. On the other hand, Lossky identifies too one-sidedly the spirituality of the Orthodox Church with Palamism. Finally, Lossky's rejection of a human imitation of Christ goes against the whole spiritual teaching of the Fathers. Contemporary authorities on patristics have clearly pointed that out.

[4] *Alexandre Boukharev* by E. Behr-Sigel has recently appeared in Paris.

[5] A Romanian writer, now deceased, has drawn up a bibliography dealing with the prayer of Jesus, in the review *Contacts* in 1974. It can be obtained from the editors, 43, rue du Fer-à-Moulin, Paris. This compilation is exhaustive and erudite rather than discerning and enlightening.

[6] The theologian C. Yannaras was a most violent adversary of Zoe, seeing in it a fringe movement, mainly lay, and—supreme criticism in the mouth of Yannaras—"pietistic".

[7] The Marian and penitent spirituality of La Salette played a considerable part in a whole religious group of Jewish, Russian and French writers (Bloy, Maritain, Massignon, Fumet, Lossky). It would be interesting to write its history.

[8] A detailed history of Orthodox influence in England would show how active and fruitful was the spiritual "mission" of N. Zernov, whose name is closely linked with the Fellowship of St. Alban and St. Sergius. Zernov did practically everything in this matter. We must also refer to the great success obtained by the talks, writings and broadcasts of Metropolitan Anthony of Sourozh among non-Orthodox as much as, and possibly more than, with the Orthodox themselves. His teaching on prayer is also a call to prayer which has found an unexpected and sometimes fascinated audience. The Oxford scholar, Archimandrite K. T. Ware, is spreading a form of hesychasm which is serious, restrained and discrete.

[9] The interest in ikons is developing particularly in Paris, centred round the artist and writer L. Ouspensky. He is assuredly a master in this subject. Some criticisms might be made of his writings concerning the exact theological meaning of the ikon, but a great enthusiasm for a great work may explain some exaggerations.

[10] The Orthodox Pentecostal movement in America, inspired especially by the theologian C. Ashanin, has already organised several congresses or conferences and published a periodical, LOGOS.

[11] The book by Archbishop Athenagoras, *The Thyateira Confession* (London, 1975), published with full approval of the Ecumenical Patriarch as a general introduction to Orthodoxy, deserves and will certainly obtain in Orthodox and non-Orthodox circles very serious consideration and discussion.